CW01304051

The Early Life of

Miss Anne Lister

& the Curious Tale of

Miss Eliza Raine

Patricia L Hughes

Hues Books Ltd

ISBN 978-1-909275-06-5

© Patricia Hughes 24th November 2015

Illustrations: Manuscripts from the Anne Lister archives in Calderdale Archives, Halifax, West Yorkshire; photograph by the author.

Dedicated to my late husband Paul who brought so much good into my life.

"It is a case of conscience … how far may be practised the liberty of chronicling conversations, or perpetuating domestic incidents."

Quarterly Review, October 1820, Page 403, quoted in Anne Lister's Diary on 5th February 1821.

Table of Contents

Introduction

1789 - 1803

1804

1806

1807

1808

1809

1810

1811

1812

1813

1814

1815

1816

1817

1819

1820

1825

1831 - 1840

Notes

Introduction

Until the middle of the eighteenth century marriage in Britain was a private affair with virtually no recognition by the state. During the early 19th century the industrial revolution brought public attention to social and financial problems. Clandestine affairs, forced marriage and related crimes like unmarried pregnancy led to several new laws, so that by 1836 all marriages were licenced and banns had to be announced in the parish church. Before 1861 girls could be procured fraudulently without any penalty at law. Twelve was the age of consent for a girl, so heiresses were regularly abducted and forced into marriage for their fortunes. Girls with less wealth were often seduced or raped. Many were left with no alternative but life on the streets. There was a serious problem of prostitution combined with a burgeoning of unwanted illegitimate children and female suicide or madness. From 1861 new laws prevented fraudulent procurement and seduction of young girls, but not until 1885 were all girls under 21 protected from such abuse.

Anne Lister and Eliza Raine were both born in 1791. Anne's diaries were written first on scraps of paper, later in notebooks and then exercise books, and from 1826 until her death in 1840 in quarto manuscript books. Eliza's were much more brief and in exercise books. Letters were often '*crossed*' or written over twice, the second set of writing at right angles to the first. Because paper was very expensive, writing was usually tiny, cramped and abbreviated (e.g. '*tho', 'thru', 'Scarbro'* etc. Going = *go.g*; they = *y.ey* etc.) and written on both sides of the paper. Many papers were torn, stained or crumpled; sealing wax had often ripped them and ink had often faded or spread. There were no consistent rules of spelling or punctuation (not until the introduction of compulsory state schools in 1870). Handwriting was copperplate. Punctuation was mostly non-existent and full stops were not commonly used; a dash was used to show the end of each 'sentence' with occasional commas in between. Capital letters only indicated importance, e.g. 'Mother'.

Much of the correspondence between Anne and Eliza was in code, probably invented by Eliza to make their writing inaccessible to others because they were in love with each other. Both knew it by heart and used it freely. It uses Latin, Greek, punctuation, mathematical and zodiac symbols, with variations for double letters and names. Their diaries contain exact times and dates, descriptions of clothes, daily routines, furniture, people and places, political events, estate management, meteorological reports and fascinating descriptions of everyday life, and their letters were neatly filed by name and date. The coded passages remained a dark secret for two centuries. Details have been transcribed and punctuation added, and my aim throughout has been to preserve the original meaning.

All Anne Lister's papers are SH:7/ML/ in the reference system used by Calderdale Archives, Halifax, West Yorkshire. Her diaries are SH:7/ML/1-26, and her miscellaneous papers are SH:7/ML/E. Eliza Raine's letters and diaries, originally held either by Anne Lister, or by William Duffin after he took charge of Eliza's estate, are SH:7/ML/A. On his death the second Mrs Duffin, née Miss Marsh, inherited them and later gave them back to Anne Lister. In 1923 all her papers, including notebooks, diaries, legal and estate records and letters to and from herself, were donated to Halifax Library. Classification marks are given whenever possible. Other sources used included the Mormons' International Genealogical Index; Register of Births, Marriages and Deaths; Dictionary of National Biography; Borthwick Institute, York; Shibden Hall Folk Museum, Halifax; York City Archives; India Office, London; Clifton Hospital Archives, York; and Jonathan Grey Solicitors of York.

1789 - 1802

James Raine left Yorkshire in 1745 for service with the East India Company as an apprentice army surgeon. While imprisoned during the Mysore War he treated the Killadar's son and saved his life, so earning the privilege of establishing his own surgery for staff and inmates. But when he was finally set free Lord Liverpool for the EIC refused to pay compensation for the use of Raine's resources until forced to do so at law. In the row that ensued the post of Head Surgeon at Madras Hospital, including responsibility for the town's public health, went to Raine's junior colleague, William Duffin.

Duffin and his wife, both from York, lived in Choultry Plain, a wealthy professional suburb not far from the affluent banana plantation with outhouses inhabited by Raine, his Indian wife and their two daughters. Jane and Eliza were half English, half Indian; their parents were married locally though not registered in England. Both army surgeons from the home country, Duffin and Raine were well respected, well-paid representatives of the East India Company and the British Empire; they took their social duties seriously and became good friends on a personal level.

In 1797 Duffin retired to Yorkshire and on leaving he nominated Raine as his successor; his friend was pleased to accept. However in 1800 Raine realised he was terminally ill and quickly set sail for England to settle his affairs, but he never reached his native soil again.[1] He died halfway through the six-month voyage and was buried at sea.

In the event of his death he had requested his accompanying servant to contact William Duffin in York. Raine's will ordered 20,000 Star Pagodas to be held in trust "for the maintenance and education of my beloved daughters Jane Elizabeth and Eliza Raine"[2]. Each Star Pagoda, issued by the East India Company, was gold worth approximately 8 shillings in contemporary English currency, meaning £4000 for each girl; each was to receive it at 21 or on marriage. His three trustees were William Duffin, Lady Mary Crawfurd, Raine's niece in Pontefract, and his bankers Thomas Coutts and Coutts Trotter of London. His brother James Raine in Scarborough was left £25 per annum – plenty to keep a workman and his family - and Lady Crawfurd was left £170 per annum.[3] As his executor Duffin set sail to Madras immediately in 1801 despite his years. It was a six-month journey each way to collect Jane and Eliza and bring them back to their father's home.

Raine left his wife the house, banana plantation and servants, perhaps because she would have no more contact with her daughters; she was never mentioned again in letters, diaries or recorded conversations. Her name is unknown. She received a pension "in pursuance of an undertaking of his to pay her 10 pagodas per month for her life", but died in July 1802 about a year after the girls had left. The cause is not recorded.[4]

As well as leaving their mother in summer 1801, Jane and Eliza also said goodbye to local colour, sunshine, heat and customs for England and their father's family. After six months on board they arrived in London in mid-winter just after Christmas 1802 aged 13 and 11 years old. Duffin put them into a small Tottenham boarding school for foreign girls, where Eliza wrote out the timetable and a list of all the students.[5]

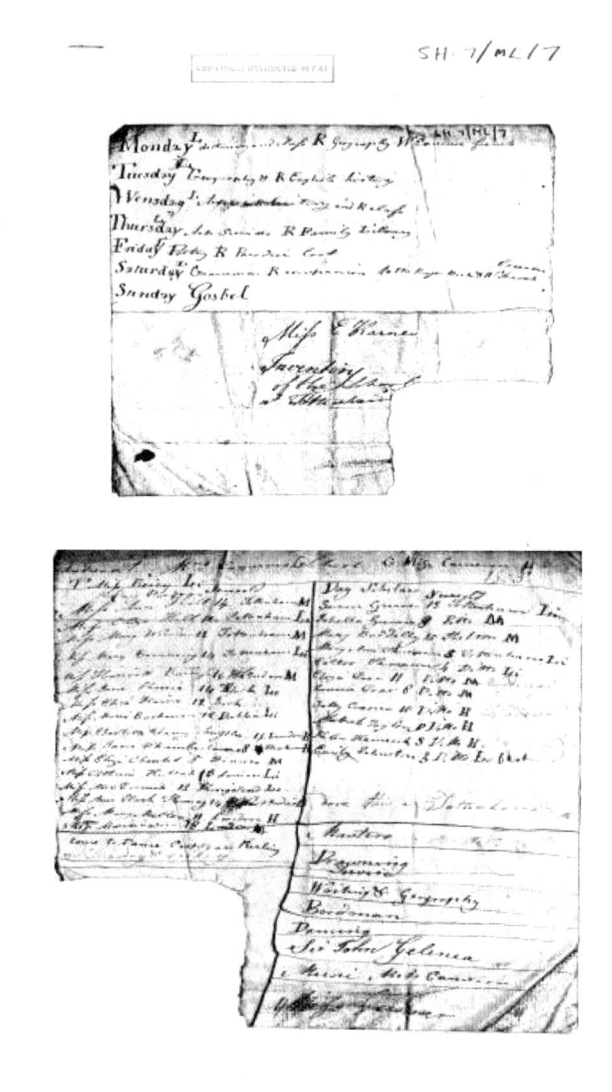

1804

Two years later in 1804 aged 15 and 13 they moved to York, where Duffin and his wife lived, to attend the Manor School. Duffin's wife was bed-ridden by now, so he engaged Miss Marsh, a governess, to look after them.

The school, for local girls with wealthy parents, was in the city next to the grounds of the mediaeval manor house. Jane lived with Mr and Mrs Duffin while attending as a day pupil and Eliza was 13 and a boarder. As the only foreigner, the only girl with dark features and black hair, and being illegitimate, it was probably difficult to arrange where she slept6. All the other girls slept in two dormitories on the first floor above the classrooms. There was just one other girl called Anne Lister, described by her brother John in a letter to his uncle James Lister as a "parlor Boarder at the Mannor, York"7, sleeping alone in an attic room called the 'slope'. However Anne was happy for Eliza to join her in the slope and Eliza was happy to accept. Before long they had a flourishing friendship. Anne wrote out the weekly timetable8.

Monday - From eight till nine Writing and Accompts
From nine till half after ten Practice
Till twelve Draw
Till one read
From three till six Geometry, Astronomy, Geography and Heraldry

Tuesday – From six in the morning till eight
And from nine till ten Geometry, Astronomy, Geography and Heraldry
From ten till half after eleven Practice
From half after eleven till one writing and accompts

Wednesday the same as Monday

Thursday from eight till half after ten Geometry, Astronomy, Geography and Heraldry
Till Twelve Practice
Till one writing and Accompts
From three till four read

Both thirteen-year-olds were intelligent and above the age of consent9. In those days a girl with a fortune was an asset because when she married her fortune was automatically transferred to her husband. Knowledge of different families and their economic fortunes was an important part of a girl's general knowledge.

Anne was a bright, active, attractive girl from a well-off, well-established landed family in Halifax. But her branch of the family had very little money, and being a girl with two older brothers and third in line to inherit, she was not expecting any. Her aunt (also called Anne) was paying for her schooling and she was probably the poorest of all the boarders, which may have been one reason for her attic bedroom. The most she could hope for in future was a substantial dowry from her relatives, that is, a lump of money to buy her a husband of her family's choice. After that as a wife she expected no legal identity and no right to own anything, even her children. She expected like every other married woman to lose all autonomy and independence, and become legally and socially just part of her husband.10

Eliza's different circumstances made her quieter and more reticent, but she faced the same prospect of being married off by her English family. In contrast to Anne, she and her sister had each inherited a fortune. Eliza had an uncle and a cousin in Yorkshire, but they were white English people she didn't know well, and neither of them knew the world she had come from or her personally. Enslavement within marriage was just as horrific to her.

Anne had another reason for not wanting to get married. She had always throughout her entire life thought of herself as a boy, acted like a boy and spoken like a boy. She saw girls as a different, attractive sex. That was the main reason she had her own room at school. Now in puberty she had feelings more appropriate to a man.

Every evening the two girls, both alienated from the others, slept in the same bed in the small, unheated attic room and confided about their schoolwork, families and personal problems, so their friendship grew deep and serious. Each had what the other craved: Anne, bereft of money, saw that Eliza possessed enough to make her independent; lonely Eliza was envious of Anne's well-respected, stable family. And when Anne put her arm around Eliza in their bedroom, the beautiful, exotic Indian girl responded.

Sometime in late 1804, after about six months together, they pledged marriage to each other earnestly and bindingly by exchanging rings and solemn promises. Anne was the husband with greatest authority, social contacts and social ambitions, while Eliza, as wife, had a steadying influence on wayward Anne and possessed all the money they needed to survive.

So that they could speak freely to one another during lessons they invented a secret code. Eliza probably invented it with Anne's assistance, since she was more proficient at language having learnt at least two Indian ones and English.

1806

They were not challenged until two years after their affair had begun; the two fifteen-year-olds were caught sending parcels to each other. No further details are known about what they contained. Anne's letters tell us that her aunt was summoned to the school and told that her niece had been misbehaving. Anne was asked to leave at once; Eliza could stay on to finish her schooling. The reasons behind this were not stated. However financially speaking Eliza was much richer – potentially – than Anne, and her guardian, Mr Duffin, was well known and respected in York, while Anne's family lived in Halifax. Anne was told that she was not welcome at the school while Eliza was there, but she could return if she so wished after Eliza had left the school.

During the following summer both girls stayed at Anne's home, Ellen Royd in Halifax, just as they had the previous year. Anne's parents didn't mind them sharing a bed, and when Eliza went back to school in the autumn their relationship continued, in secret as far as the school was concerned. From when she left in August Anne recorded every letter and parcel to or from Eliza in a small notebook in secret code.

Monday August 11th Eliza left us.

Had a letter from her on Wednesday morning by Mr Ratcliffe the 13th inst.

Wrote to her on Thursday 14th by Mr Lund.

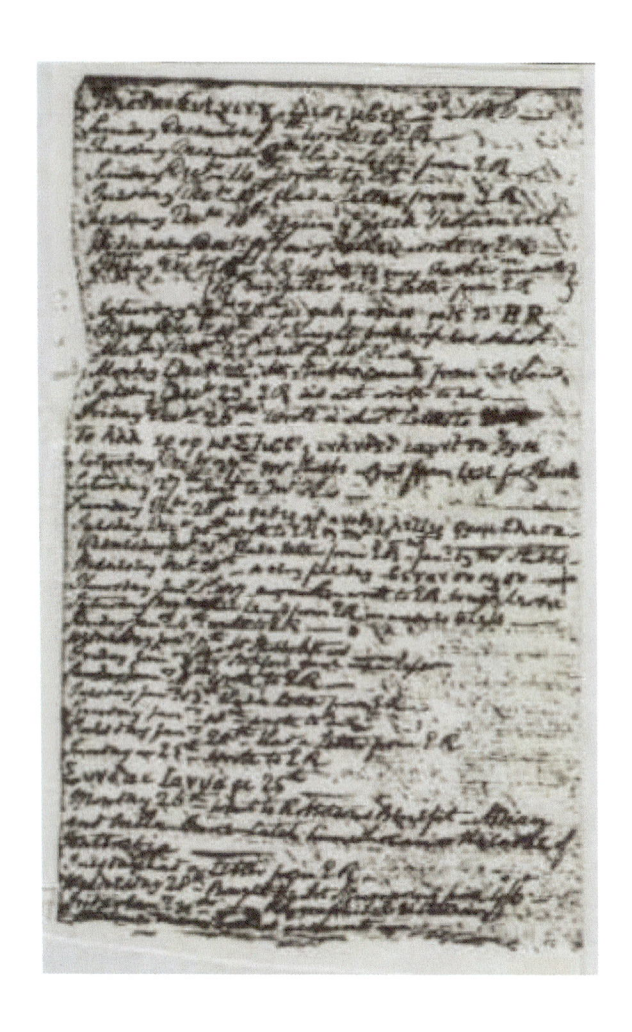

My dearest Eliza,

So anxious am I to know whether you are comfortable and how you arrived at the Manor that I can scarcely persuade myself to have patience to wait for a day or two for your ever welcome Epistle, which though a poor substitute for your company will give unspeakable pleasure to me whose only study is your happiness. I hope my dear girl you are sufficiently a philosopher to make you content in all stations and to consider everything for the best and our parting as a circumstance pre-ordained for our future and greater comfort. Ah! dear Liz I'm preaching up doctrine that is of little service to me as distracted to lose you I sigh and lament me in vain fully verifying the old proverb that the more you have the more you would have. I study much to stay my grief and think on your letters for relief. Anne Lister11

Wrote to her again on Sunday 17th put into the post office at Leeds on the Monday following. That evening the 18th had a parcel from her Music Letter & Lavender.

Had a letter Wednesday August 20th answered on the 21st.

Sunday 24th wrote to E.R. put into the post on Monday.

Wednesday 27th had a letter from her in answer to two.

Friday 28th rec'd a parcel from E.R. by W. Lund.

Sunday 30th wrote to E.R. in answer to ten sheets by Mr Lund.

Tuesday 9th had a letter from her.

Wednesday 10th had a letter from E.R.

Friday 12th had a letter from E.R.

Thursday 11th wrote to E.R. in answer to hers of the 10th.

Sunday Sepbr 14th wrote to E.R. by my Uncle & Aunt J. Lister going to Hull on the same day, a short note to Miss Hargrave enclos'd with 3 P. handkerchiefs 1 Slip in a Parcel with my Letter to E.R. in answer to one from her on Saturday 13th by Mr Vastlet enclosing me a Cornelian Brooch.

At first she made no other entries, but Anne's record of postage soon began to metamorphose into a record of events.12

Monday August 25th 1806 rode with Mr Mitchell to Bacup the first time I ever was out of Yorkshire.

Tuesday Sepbr 16th had a letter from E.R. in answer to mine by my Uncle & Aunt by the Post, they being at Hull.

Wednesday rode with Mr Mitchell to Fixby through Elland, Rastrix and Brighouse. On that day was the Oratoria at Elland Wednesday Sepbr 19th 1806.

Sunday Sepbr 21st wrote to E.R. in answer to a packet by my Uncle & Aunt Lister returned from Hull.

Sunday Sepbr 28th wrote to E.R. on a large sheet filled on all sides.

Tuesday 30th had a letter from E.R.

Octbr Friday 3rd wrote a note to E.R. by Lund to Tadcaster by Hull to York enclosed with "Je suis Lindor, a Welch Ayr" and the following written to Raine:

1st, Do not play Je suis Lindor for fear you sh'd take the infection

2nd Ah! One sad moment when you're not aware

May plunge you in the deep abyss of care.

3rd With love & best thanks, Yours, Lister.

Sunday Octbr 5th wrote to E.R.

Tuesday Octbr 7th had a letter from E.R.

Sunday Octbr 12th wrote to E.R.

Tuesday Octbr 14th had a letter from E.R.

Friday Octbr 10th attended one of Mr Dalton's Lectures13 and was well entertain'd, went with Mr Joseph Lister and Mr Nicholls.

Monday Octbr 13th attended another of Dalton's Lectures, Galvanism Went with Mr J.L. & Mr N.

Friday Octbr 10th got Henry's Chemistry.

Octbr Thursday 16th Mr Stubbs14 came in the morning.

Octbr 17th 18th 20th & 21st did not attend Mr Knight.15

21st Octbr had a letter from E.R.

Sunday Octbr 19th wrote to E.R.

Sunday Octbr 26th wrote to E.R.

Monday Octbr 27th in the evening Mr Midgley came.

Tuesday Octbr 28th had a letter from E.R. Mr Stubbs left us by the coach. Mane.16

Thursday Octbr 30th Mr Midgley left us. Mane.

Friday Octbr 31st & Saturday Novbr 1st did not attend Mr Knight.

Monday Novbr 3rd wrote a very short letter to E.R., 1st side only filled.

Tuesday Novbr 4th had a letter from E.R.

Monday evening Novbr 3rd and Tuesday morning wrote another letter to E.R. by my Mother who left Halifax for Weighton17 Novbr 4th by the mail18. Also sent to E.R. by my Mother my hair woven into the words Lord Remember David & Mr Cammage's [book] March.

Sunday noon November 2nd 1806

Sunday Novbr 9th wrote to E.R.

Tuesday Novbr 11th had a letter from E.R.

Friday Novbr 7th my Father went to Weighton.

Thursday Novbr 13th My Father arrived here from Weighton. Monday Novbr 17th wrote to E.R.

Wednesday Novbr 19th had a parcel from E.R. by my Mother on her return from Weighton. 1st snow at Halifax.

Sunday Novbr 23rd wrote to E.R.

Thursday Novbr 27th had 3 sheets from E.R. in a parcel for my Mother. Went to Mr Stopford's19 1st concert in a Habit skirt20 & was much stared at and well quizzed as an original. Care despised on my part. The Music of Women & divers Instruments continued until half past 10.

Sunday Novbr 30th wrote to E.R.

Tuesday December 2nd very snowy day.

Rebecca Lister's adopted Irish son Mr Stubbs was proposed as a match with Eliza, as she had a considerable dowry and was Anne's best friend. But Eliza, having secretly married Anne, didn't want to meet him. Anne did not encourage her to do so either. Perhaps she was jealous. So Mr Stubbs was sent to meet Eliza in York, far away from Halifax, to propose marriage.

Tuesday Decbr 16th had a letter from E.R. Begun the Greek Testament.

Wednesday Decbr 17th my Father wrote to E.R.

Thursday Decbr 18th E.R. wrote to my Father in answer.

Friday Decbr 19th Mr Knight broke up his school.

Monday Decbr 22 went to Mr Knight's. Mr Stubbs came from Ireland.

Tuesday Decbr 23rd E.R. did not write to me.

Friday Decbr 26th wrote a short letter to E.R. to tell her of Mr Stubb's intended jaunt to York.

Saturday Decbr 27th Mr Stubbs went from here to Thirsk. Went to Mr K's.

Sunday Decbr 28th my Father had another letter from Eliza.

Tuesday Decbr 30th wrote to E.R. by Mr Lund.

Wednesday November 31st a very fine day. Begun Sokrates

1807

But as Eliza had turned Mr Stubbs down, she then had to confront her 'mother'.
Thursday Jany 1st 1807 my Mother wrote to E.R. to ask her over.
Saturday my Mother heard from E.R. in answer to hers.

January 2d 1807

Dear Mrs Lister,

I received yours this moment and am rather confounded at your stile but I cease my surprise and to the best of my power will answer your (to me) odd questions… forgive the haste in which this is written. I have written to Captain Lister, excuse me saying more. Believe me ever to be as I profess, I love you with my usual affection and do not grieve me by writing so short a letter for the future … Tell your daughter Anne with my best love I hope she will write me longer letters for the future, that I beg, employed as she is she will manage to dedicate a few more minutes to one forever her sincere friend, I shall write to her on Monday. I hope your family are well, present my remembrances to all, not forgetting Mr Stubbs, in which my Sister joins. Keep up your spirits dear Mrs L., if circumstances occasionally happen to disturb you, forget all with the usual generosity of your heart, forgive me but you know not my anxiety for yours & all real happiness for believe me I am your affectionate Daughter. … In you I will confide as to a dear Parent & to Mr Lister, I will act the part to your children as if they were very relations; excuse me if ever my actions are erroneous, if I thoughtlessly commit a fault & cause you regret pass it over & know my nature is not perfect. My eagerness for you to know & keep in mind my thoughts has led me to enlarge thus. My motives are good & therefore I again entreat you to be lenient. Mr Stubbs gratified me as much with a good account of you all …he appears truly amiable. I hope to hear from you soon & entreating you earnestly to consider me as I profess I remain forever your affectionate

& grateful Daughter

Eliza Raine

Mr & Mrs Duffin

*desire their kind Compliments to you, Mr Lister and the rest of the family.*21

June Monday 15th wrote to E.R. Had a Holiday
Tuesday 16th had a letter from E.R.
Wednesday 17th had a packet from E.R. by young Priestleys
Thursday 18 got out of Isocrates

Saturday 20th begun Xenophon
Sunday June 14th began mux mane22
Friday June 19th Mr K school broke up that day
Saturday 20th went to Mr Knight's
Thursday 25th wrote to E.R. sent on Friday 26th
Wednesday 24th and Thursday 25th both the banks stopped. Swain's was shut up and Ingram's only open to give answers without doing any business. Sylvester's bank at Huddersfield and Ingram's at Wakefield stopped same time.

Why Eliza so wan and pale
List'ning as if to mis'ry's tale
Why shew such tumults 'stead of rest
Indication of a good breast
Alas I reply I'm in love
From me has fled my sweet love
'Tis thus why I so oft do mourn
Ah! he my faithful heart does scorn.
Thou most cruel of thy sad sex
That bear'st the noble arms of sex
Far from me take your winding path
Or stay to kindle still my wrath.

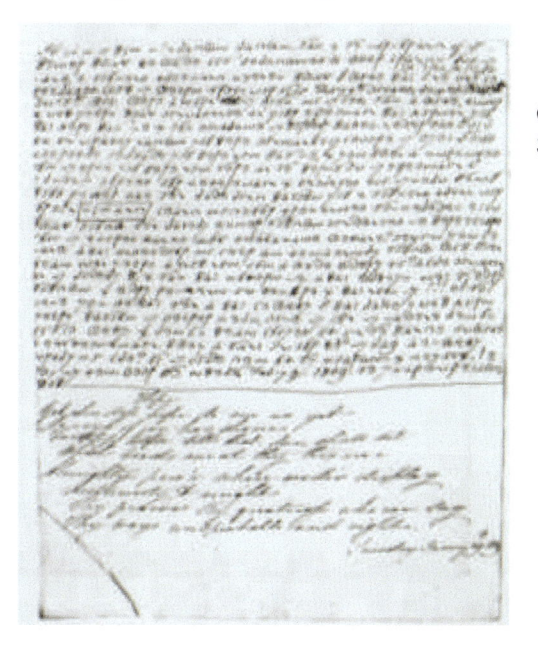

Both were very much in love with each other. When Eliza returned alone to the Manor School in December 1807 she felt very lonely.

1808

Friday Jany 1st Went to Mr Knight
Sunday 3rd wrote to E.R.
Tuesday 5th had a letter from E.R. Mr Lund went to York. Mad.
Thursday 7th drank tea with Miss Alexander
Friday 8th afternoon Began 23
Sunday 10th wrote E.R.
Thursday 14th had a letter from E.R.
Saturday 16th went to Mr K.
Monday 18th drank tea at Northgate. 24 My uncle Joe gave me decem/sex. 25
Thursday 21st went to Mr K. Had a party of gentlemen. Sent 2 small sheets to E.R. that ought to have gone by Mr Priestleys by Post.
Friday 22nd call'd upon Miss Alexander, Miss Ramsden & Miss Mellings. Miss Ramsden drank tea with us.
Saturday 23rd wrote a short letter by Mr Priestleys to E.R.
Thursday 28th Jan had a letter from E.R.
Sunday 31st wrote to E.R. Drank tea with Miss A.
Sunday Febry 1st Miss A. began music. 26
Sunday Febry 1st 1808
My dear Eliza,

I shall begin with telling you that I cannot say much this week. However I will not waste time in making apologies, therefore to proceed. I thank you much for your last long letter, which I wish it were in my power to answer more worthily, but such pleasure I trust will not always be out of my reach as it has been of late; the idea of seeing you so soon can alone reconcile me to it, but in this most comfortable thought I find every needful consolation. I am glad that you esteem yourself so happily situated and equally so that you think me as affectionate as ever; I assure you Eliza I am very steady in my attachments, and though not deemed of an

affectionate disposition, I feel that I can be strongly attached to my dear and kind friend E.R. You still give me an unfavourable account of your health, indeed I cannot get the better of a thousand fears concerning you, nor can I forget that tender yet painful anxiety which is to me the greatest proof how much I love you, but I see it is in vain to tell of my solicitude since you are so surrounded with gaiety that you have not had time to think of your own complaints much less those of your friend.

I daresay Mrs L. is in no great hurry for the worsteds, but when I see her I will mention what you say. I have not heard my Mother speak of going to Weighton in March. You make good resolves concerning your studies, and I hope you have as good a mind to keep them. You have had your share of Valentines. I had one, from whom I cannot guess, in singularity somewhat like one of yours, I think:

"All hail! Thou beauteous charming fair
Whose great designs thy noble mind declare;

*Permit a poet male in humble lays
To sing to thee an Amazonian praise.
With thy great Drum* oh! lead thy troops to war
And let its dreadful sound be heard afar;
Thy needle, distaff, puddings and thy pies,
Thy much loved cheesecakes and thy curds despise;
Let noble objects emulate thy mind
By grammar rules and classic laws refin'd;
Let great Maonedes with sounding lyre
Or softer Virgil all thy thoughts inspire.
In thy charmed soul let fam'd Anacreon sing
Or Roman Horace touch the lyric string.
With these acquirements thou wilt lovers gain
And future ages will immortalise thy name. Eugenio.
alluding to my beating the Drum which you will recollect that I sometimes used to do …

I know nothing more dismal than the tolling of a death-bell therefore do not wonder that it should incline you to melancholy, but pleasing thought! if we live well we may joyfully expect death that will make to cease all care and trouble. Good night my dear friend and may you not wound the heart of that one to whom every pleasure is imperfect which Eliza does not share. L.

*N.B. For your information I give you a translation of the two Latin ornaments of my Valentine:
Latet anguis in herba – Deep in the grass the wary snake lies hid.
Contra quam sentis solet Ironia Jocari – You see against whom Irony is wont to joke.*27

*Tuesday 2nd Miss A. a lesson
Wednesday 3rd Miss A. a lesson. Begun Mane.
Thursday 4th had a letter from E.R.
Friday 5th Miss A. had a lesson and Saturday 6th too.
Sunday 7th dined at S.H.*28*Drank tea with Miss A. Monday 8th in the morning wrote a short letter to E.R., also gave Miss A. a lesson and drank tea.
Monday 8th began a quadratic. Give Miss A. a lesson regularly Mon. Wednes. Friday
Thursday 11th had a letter from E.R.
Saturday 13th begun Euclid
Sunday 14th wrote to E.R.
Monday 15th had a Valentine.
Friday 19th had a letter from E.R.
Saturday 20th dined and spent the whole day with Miss A. looking over books. Play'd two rubbers with Lewis A.*29
*Thursday 25th Had a Letter from E.R.
Friday 26th Miss A.*30 *went to the Royd*31*. Till now every lesson one excepted and every Sunday one excepted from after Sunday Feb 7th drank tea with Miss A.
Wednesday 24th Finished 4 lib*32 *Horace's Odes.*

20

Thursday 25th Finished 2 lib of Homer.
Friday 26th Dined at Mr Mitchell's, met there Mrs Dickinson, Miss Bagnold & Mr Bradford. Had a Holiday.

Miss E. Raine,

Mr Duffin's Esqr.33

Micklegate, York   *Halifax Sunday Febry 28th 1808*

My dear Eliza,

After musing long on subjects oft revolved in my unsettled mind, I would at length recollect my widely scattered thoughts to engage them more worthily and fondly turn them to my much loved friend, to you Eliza, from whom I weekly find some newly added token of regard, your affectionate remembrance of the happiness which we have mutually experienced in each other's society casts over my soul a momentary gloom and whilst it bids me think how much I gained when first I gained your friendship, bids me think how much I lost when conscious of my loss I lost Eliza but it seems as if I had forgotten that this strain must be very unpleasing --- I am glad that you have been for a while free from gaiety; you tell me that you have staid quietly at home for nearly the third of a Week, which is equal to two days and eight hours. So long tranquillity is I daresay to you very unusual but perhaps less ungrateful.

I think your partiality for shells is the forerunner of a partiality for other natural curiosities and hence perchance we may one day trace the origin of your turning student in natural philosophy. At present, my dear friend, I have little hope of being able to make any worthy addition to your cabinet, however I will not forget how I may oblige you. I should like much to hear what shells you have already gotten – you do not tell me half enough about yourself.

I wish to know everything that you do, what you like & dislike etc. Perhaps whilst at Red House34 you will spend some time on Botany, or is this not one of your favourite studies? From what I can gather from your Epistles I think you are most fond of French and Painting. You do not say when Mr Bell35 has fixed to attend you; does he say much in favour of the mathematics or does he rather persuade you to give your attention to other pursuits? What are you about in Arithmetic?

I cannot agree with you in thinking that you are become stupid and that every exertion ceased with our separation for I think that you improved yourself much more after I left school than you did when I was with you, your Letters are proof positive of this. I much wish, my dear Eliza, that you would forbear any apology for your style of writing when it happens to be grave, you well know that whatever your feelings may be at the moment when you write, mine when I read them are in consonance.

Your Valentine is of so romantic a turn that I have not kept it secret, you are more fortunate in finding out the author of it than I shall be with regard to mine, though dated Halifax.

We must have troops in the West Indies and if they take care of themselves I do not see why they may not return from thence as well as from any other place especially if they be young men ---

I am sorry that you have reason to suspect your sister of corresponding with Mr B,36 but I hope you will endeavour to take it more indifferently, for it is time that we cease to lament a thing when we cannot remedy it ---

I trust as the summer approaches Mrs Duffin will gain strength of body and Miss Raine strength of mind, to both of whom I beg to be kindly remembered Mrs Swann is certainly an amiable woman and happy are you who share her kindness --- remember me to all my friends particularly to my Aunt Anne and the Manners when you write to them, how do they enjoy their altered situation? ---

I may fairly retort the charge of concluding my last Letter rather dismally, why does my dear Eliza bid adieu and bid me believe her a most affectionate though sometimes unhappy friend? What melancholy thought; what sad remembrance bade Eliza call herself unhappy? Ah my dear let me share thy grief, still let my joys and sorrows be known by thine. It was once thus and why not be so now? But do I hear thee say it cannot be? If this be separation, unhappy moment when I saw you last, unhappy moment when I see thee next. L.   37

When she left school two years earlier Jane Raine went to Doncaster to live with her cousin Lady Crawfurd, but unfortunately found her difficult to live with and returned after about a year to the Duffin's house. Feeling uncomfortably surplus in York, Jane often stayed with her uncle James Raine and his family in Seamer near Scarborough38.

On the coach journey back whilst changing horses in Malton Jane made the acquaintance of Henry Boulton, a handsome cadet on leave from Calcutta. He talked to her about India; she enjoyed his company; then he proposed marriage. Jane was almost twenty-one and due to inherit her fortune; financial and social independence left her feeling very insecure; her sister might get married to someone else and be lost to her forever. She needed security.

Henry Boulton was about a year older than Jane, born on the 8th April 1787 in Malton, halfway between York and Scarborough. As a fourth son he had no fortune; most of his family's money would go on a good dowry for the eldest girl and a good education for the eldest boy. Henry had to earn his own income in the church or army, and until he did he couldn't marry or have a family, even if he wanted one. He had joined the Madras Infantry as a cadet in 1807 and promotion was not available unless he paid for it. His only alternatives were to find an heiress to marry, or to cheat or steal from someone else.

But Henry knew Jane's home country and said he loved her. Therefore she accepted his proposal without hesitation, despite a severe warning from Mr Duffin. They married hastily on 21st of May 1808 at Trinity Church, right opposite Mr Duffin's house in Micklegate, and set off straight away to Calcutta. Eliza was distraught; now that Jane had become Mrs Henry Boulton she never expected to see her sister again. She became depressed.

21 Mch 1808

Miss E. Raine, Wm. Duffins Esqr., Micklegate York   Halifax – Sunday March 1808

My dear Eliza   I assure you I am heartily glad that you are really quite recovered – long may you be in good health and still longer may you not voluntarily bring on sickness by imprudence – when you are with me I hope you will take a long walk every day get up early in a morning and go to bed regularly at an early hour not do as I fear you do now – it is a trite saying but nevertheless true that Early to bed early to rise makes a man healthy wealthy and wise – now let us see the truth of this confirmed in you –

Though you had a disappointment when you last wrote it did not seem to affect your good humour towards me indeed my dear Eliza it is long since you have written to me otherwise than in the greatest good humour which justice does not always demand but I will hope that such kindness will in future be deserved yet how you deprecate unfortunate man! Can Eliza for the fault of one involve the whole sex in common contempt? No it cannot be – let me say something in their vindication but perhaps it is not my business therefore I pause - … or I would wish to pry into your secret thoughts –

I am glad to hear you say that you hope we shall again spend days as happy as those already spent I wish we may but Hope says no such thing to me do not let this cast a gloom over your bright prospects perhaps I view our happiness through a concave mirror – affection is not wanting on my part to make us most happy but something I know not what disturbs me –

Since I wrote to you I have spent some time very agreably in France from Dover I proceeded to Calais and from thence to Paris in my route I passed through the pleasant seaport of Boulogne and not mentioning other less interesting places through the city of Amiens whose noble cathedral I saw with wonder and regret and as I passed through the once Elysian Chantilly contemplated with horror the effects of the late revolution39 whilst viewing the mutilated chateaus of this still delightful place – at length I am arrived at Paris.

To keep you no longer in suspense I have been reading Redhead Yorke's tour in France in two octavo volumes40 a very good publication I cannot forbear mentioning Madame

Therouanne a young fanatical girl who would have been one of the finest women in France had she less despised those softer graces and winning charms which she really eminently possessed insomuch that one young man was so fond of her as to offer marriage upon which she put a pistol to his heart and threatened to shoot him if ever he mentioned the subject again – this poor fellow! damped his hopes but not his love for Madame T - headed a body of Pikemen against the king on the memorable 10th of August and was distinguished for her bravery and presence of mind –

When Mr Yorke was asked to breakfast with this Lady the first things which he saw on entering her room were a pike, a dagger a sabre a brace of pistols, on the floor about a hundred volumes and pamphlets on her table the Journals de Paris on her bed L'ami du peuple by Marat and suspended from the chimney-piece the bonnet rouge –

From Mr Yorke's description of Paris it was at that time 1802 one of the most dissipated licentious places that can be imagined – some scenes he says would have made the hair of the most hardened Libertine in England stand on end and speaking of their libidinous books he says that if a pen had been put into the hands of Satan or the evil genius of mankind he could not have written worse – There was even a common prostitute deified and worshipped – What does my Eliza think? Come have I not said enough – have I not worn out your patience? But you know me you know my wandering mind sometimes strays beyond the horizon of my native place but "my heart untravell'd fondly turns to thee"   L

Did your Sister take courage and go to Mrs Hunter's rout?41 Pardon me for I never till this moment thought of the Lyre or worsteds -

Eliza's losing her sister was, of course, sad, but to be expected. Anne was sympathetic and invited her to her parents' house in Halifax again for the summer. Eliza started writing her diary again, as she always did when with Anne:

Aug 3rd 1808 Felix. Mr Walker & Miss Fitz. dined here. Went to walk at the Baths. Mr H Priestley dined here with Mr & Miss Lister of Shibden Hall & Mr Watkinson.

August 4th Felix.

8th Sunday Wrote to Mrs Duffin, Mrs Swann, Mrs Hurst.

Left Halifax Novr 8th 1808.42

'Felix' is Latin for 'happiness', meaning they were having sex. These entries coincide with the same entries in Anne's notebook diary in August 1808. The two seventeen-year-olds spent a very happy summer in each other's company. They visited as many people as they could, including Mrs Greenup, sister of Miss Marsh, their governess in York. When September came they spent three weeks with uncle James and his family before Eliza returned to school in York.

Wednesday 23rd   Had a Letter from my Aunt Anne with a present of Dr Hunter's[43] publication of Men & Manners by the author.

Friday 25th   Had a Letter from E.R. & some worsteds to my aunt A. Wrote again to my aunt to acknowledge the book & her Letter.

Sunday 27   Wrote to E.R.

Monday 28th Had another Letter from my aunt Anne. Miss Alexander came home today ...

Tuesday 5th   Gave Miss Alexander the first lesson since her return home ...

Wednesday 20th Miss A. missed her lesson in consequence of going out to tea at Miss Hoyle's, New Road.

Thursday 21st Had a Letter from E.R.

Friday 22nd   Miss A. missed her lesson in consequence of Mr Stopford tuning the instrument.

Sunday 24th   wrote to E.R.

Wednesday 27th Wrote to my mother, No. 3 George St, Hull.

Omitted: Monday 11th my mother and father went to Weighton. My father returned Sunday morning half past 7. [44]

Anne's circle of friends in Halifax had widened. She was continuing her studies with the Reverend Knight and with two sisters called Miss Mellin at their ladies' school and meeting other pupils.

However her visits to a particular family were causing her parents a great deal of concern. To start with she began giving flute lessons to unmarried Miss Maria Alexander after her elder sister had been married off with a dowry. Of course that was acceptable for seventeen-year-old Anne; Maria was fifteen years older,[45] the daughter of elderly Robert Alexander, a local doctor.

It would have been a respectable family except that all the other siblings were unmarried men, all older than Anne. The three eldest sons were doctors and the youngest was an army captain. Anne's parents found card games and musical evenings acceptable, but "routs"[46] were not. At the Alexander household she was staying later and later.

The Lister and Alexander families did not visit socially; nevertheless Anne persuaded her Shibden Hall relatives to invite Maria Alexander to dinner. A short time later Mr Alexander the elder reciprocated and invited the Shibden Hall Listers to dinner, but they declined. To smooth over this social embarrassment Maria's aunt called on Captain Lister's family at Ellen Royd, but Rebecca refused to see her at all, Captain Lister was rude and Anne was forbidden to visit them again.

But she did. On October 21st she went there to teach the flute and took Eliza with her. In Eliza's presence Anne flirted with Maria, admitting that she was in love but without saying with whom. Then, according to Anne's diary, Eliza encouraged Anne to sit Maria on her knee and kiss her. She was making it clear to Eliza not to expect loyalty, and before long they agreed to wait longer than before to live together. Twenty-one now seemed impractical to Anne; twenty-seven seemed more realistic. A week later Eliza's summer visit drew to an end, and Anne was annoyed with her dark-skinned friend because she had become despondent and had a sharper tone:

I long to impress upon your lips all that real sincerity & warmth of affection which flows but frigidly on paper … Can these lines, once the produce of happier hours, make one tear steal down, Liz, sing a requiem to thy troubled heart? Think, think dear Liz, how gentle thou wert once and how discordant now. Think, are not the virtues spoiled?[47]

Anne paid for Eliza's box to be sent back to York, and in early November Eliza left Halifax with the thought of having to wait ten years until 1818. She wrote a love-letter to Anne from York:

"It is a sweet moonlight night; this and the murmuring of the water which we have both delighted to hear brings to my mind a thousand pleasing scenes which I hope will one day be realised. How my heart throbs for thee! (1 Feb 9th copied, letter, Decr 5th 1809) Here I turn my eyes to my bed. This I hope after a few years which confidence in your affection will shorten you will share with me and thus complete my worldly wishes. Never did I feel as on Friday night; you were continually before my eyes; I could scarcely believe you were not with me. And yet when I stretched out my arms you were not there in the warmth of my affection. I almost cursed our separation and declared to myself that I would rather die than live long without you. A thousand plans for our soon meeting, being together, presented themselves, all of which, though then likely, afterthought convinced me were absurd. But my adored since much exquisite happiness cannot yet be mine I will endeavour to bear it patiently, though how I can wait for ten years I know not. But I have every confidence in my lovely W[48] *and this will support me. I will always tell thee every thought and every remnant of desire, and will not my W. do the same? Yes she will and then I will be happy, and let us wait buoyed up on the wings of hope and expectation.*

When I think of our N[49] *my Liz I am truly happy so bless thee my love, get up thy spirits. De'r the twelfth. The year of the above 1808."*[50]

In December Anne's father had been asked if she could join Disney Alexander and Sam Dyson on a trip to Portsmouth since Maria's brother, Captain John, was unable to go. Her parents refused of course: an unmarried woman accompanying two single men could provoke a case of breach of promise.51 If she refused to act as a woman should, she would be regarded as indecent.

Anne took no notice and carried on acting like a bachelor rather than a spinster. A couple of days later she took her father's pistols, cleaned and refilled them and installed one of them in her personal desk "*to be ready if ever wanted in a hurry*".52

Then, to have an excuse for her frequent unaccompanied walks into town she undertook to paint her Aunt Lister's birdhouse at Northgate House, from where it was just a short step to the Alexander's. Nothing was said about her manly actions until one evening when Anne was walking home in the dark and met with Sam Dyson in the wood. All that she recorded in her diary was an acute sense of shame and embarrassment.53 Two days later her father, having got wind of the incident, set a curfew of 4pm.54 However it only provoked Anne: the following day her mother gave her permission to visit the Alexanders and she arrived home at 5.30pm.

In reaction Captain Lister declared the Alexander house out of bounds, but Anne went there for half an hour two days later, then every day for an hour until the twenty-fourth of December, as she gleefully records in her diary. On the twenty-eighth her parents granted her permission to stay over two nights to attend New Year festivities, and she slept in the same bed as Maria for a fortnight.

1809

At home Anne did not miss Eliza after the first month or so; now that she had no school she was enjoying her freedom. She was seventeen, masculine in all but her body, and there was no one to object any more.

Almost unrestricted she began to explore the lifestyle of a man. She wrote her first book review, on Arthur Mee's "Rhymes on Art". The same evening, unchaperoned, she played cards with Dr Disney Alexander and his friend Sam Dyson, and then went there again and again.

The crowning point came on January 4th when, still at the Alexander's, she pretended to faint and had to be revived by Disney, a doctor. Although Anne thought it very amusing her father did not. Furious about the effects on her marriage prospects and the family's reputation, he re-imposed the curfew, cancelling all of Anne's social engagements; but three days later Anne once again ignored him and spent the whole day at the Alexander's.

Unfortunately when she returned home that evening she found her aunt Anne and uncle James waiting for her. They had been there all day because she had previously agreed to spend a week with them at Shibden Hall55 – but she'd forgotten they were coming on that day. Her aunt and uncle were the financial key to her future so she had to treat them seriously.

By the end of January Eliza was anxiously enquiring if Anne was ill; she had received no word from her 'husband'. Eliza was hurt by the neglect. If Anne didn't want her any more, who else would? If she was no longer part of the Lister family, whom did she belong to? The answer was no one.

"Written at the close of day

This day has passed the hour grows nigh
That gives me peace and rest
My fire is trimmed & yet I sigh
For griefs against my breast.

This night unusual pangs sit here
Oppressive sad and deep
They're thine which vibrate in my ear
Down hither while they sleep.

They've told me how thou sigh'd and thought
And pass'd ye midnight waste
A present sympathy they brought
A balsam which I taste _ _ _

For mem'ry always mourns and weeps
To think to bring again
Those joys remembrance hoarded keeps
To soothe me in my pain.

But mem'ry thou fallacious art
Thou mock'st me with thy smile
For while I gaze upon thy part
Behold 'tis nought but guile.

But fondle thee I must and will

Thou art best loved by me
For tho' my heart thou wound'st still
No friend have I but thee "_ _ _56   Jany 30 1809
Monday

    Following a talk with her aunt and uncle Anne did not visit the Alexander's and her teenage tempestuousness became much more sensible and moderate. She resumed writing to Eliza once a week. By the time she returned to Ellen Royd her parents had spoken to the Alexanders and reached some agreement. By February aunt Anne and uncle James were regularly having dinner at Ellen Royd to encourage Anne with her studies.

    Anne had nevertheless scarred her reputation. Miss Bramley, a delicate young lady from an affluent family, enquired about a rumour concerning Anne and Captain Bourne of which her father disapproved; on being told what had happened, Miss Bramley "cut" her.57 One month later Miss Bramley was sent to a finishing school in London, and so was Miss Maria Alexander, to remove them from bad influences. Anne wrote defensively that she did not care; she was glad not to have to dress and parade like a lady.

    But the incident with Captain Bourne had to be explained to the curious. When she visited Mrs Greenup she was asked to tell what had happened, and she admitted that she had accompanied Captain Bourne to his room to see his pistols. Mrs Greenup thought the incident hilariously funny, and her husband took out his German pistols for Anne to see. Sexual impropriety had not occurred – who would have believed it of Anne? She felt like a man so she had acted like a man. That evening when she went to the theatre young George Pollard insisted on Anne using his box.58 Mrs Greenup also told her sister, Miss Marsh, Mr Duffin's governess for the Raine girls, that Anne had been accepted as a young man by other young men.

    The following Sunday Anne walked to church with the men instead of the women. Such an obvious statement was however provocative and the next day Disney made a pass at her.59 Two days later she met Captain Bourne again and, at his invitation, went back to his room again to see his "*flageolet*", and drank wine with him. He proposed a closer relationship, but she demurred, instead offering to introduce him to her parents.60 Captain Lister and Rebecca reacted with predictable fury, her father "*annoyed at the impropriety*", and her mother "*hurt*". Once again they re-imposed the curfew on the Alexander household, but they could not stop Anne being what she was.

    On the 27th March their daughter bought a pair of men's braces for herself.61

    On her 18th birthday, April 3rd, Anne was suddenly violently sick with a momentary loss of sight and great weakness, so that she had to lean on Mr Farrar, her music teacher, in order to get home. This brought Disney to her again; he declined a fee.

He then continued to make regular visits to check her health, but his prescriptions were not orthodox:

> Dr Disney called in the morning, he said as friend, to inquire after me, sayg. that there were two or three things wch he cd recommend. My mother asked him what they were & he wrote me a prescription for asafoetida pills.62

Anne's behaviour was deliberately provocative and her reputation in tatters, but she had established herself as more masculine than feminine and very daring, so locals began to refer to her as "*Gentleman Jack*". It had advantages nevertheless and paid off in May that year. In Ellen Royd older servants and family members suddenly roused her from her sleep late one night; they had heard strange sounds and were frightened. Clutching a candle Anne led the way to the attic, where she discovered that two girl servants had invited their boyfriends overnight. The boys were sent packing immediately and the girls dismissed the next day. Dauntless Anne had been chosen to protect the whole family, including her brothers; she had no problem taking control of the situation.63

What bothered Anne far more than her reputation was money. Landed families like hers did not receive much cash except rents and farm or business income, so their lifestyle was sedate and careful. They had beautiful old houses but seldom owned carriages or held parties; expensive clothes, riding for pleasure and travel were considered rare luxuries. In contrast most of Anne's friends had parents self-employed in medicine, banking or industry. The Alexanders, Rawsons, Priestleys and Crossleys were professional or industrial families with cash income and outgoings, and they had to maintain social presence with good clothes, social gatherings and new houses.

Anne felt the contrast keenly. She felt slighted by Miss Fern, who sneered when she had her mother's 'habit' cut down to fit her. She had to be careful with pocket money because her parents gave it to her erratically; she was dependent on gifts from her aunts and uncles and Eliza. In order not to offend her father such donations were made secretly. But Eliza was very rich.

Mrs Lister, Halifax   *York May 15th 180964*

My dear Mrs Lister

How much do I owe you for this happiness you have conferred on me. I need hardly say what have been my sensations since you must know my heart. Accept my thanks for forgetting so kindly my past errors and follies; & if the future should prove that my frail nature is not easily to be subdued pardon me my dear Mrs Lister & check me with a severity which I shall deserve. I was not very well a little while ago indeed I must candidly confess I thought I should soon pay the debt of nature & I assure you there it was I wished to be, at peace with all men & when I looked into my heart I found something which made me unhappy. I anxiously waited for that which you have kindly brought to pass& for which I will more warmly thank you in person.

By your kind offer I an enabled to enjoy your society this Summer My friends are very anxious I should accept it & I need hardly say how happy I am to comply Mr Duffin desires me to say on any plan I shall be glad to join you& share with you. And if you will write to me again mentioning your further determinations I will be ready by the 1st of June –

My health is almost well, I have no particular complaint but they tell me I waste away in the midst of good spirits & a large appetite, indeed I feel a general languor & debility, for a week I am well & then I relapse again into my former lassitude. I take new milk in a morning & sometimes sago at night. I daresay bathing will give me all I have lost.

I am glad to find my friend is better, you say nothing of yourself or other members of your family but I hope they are quite well. I am sorry indeed to hear of Miss Lister's indisposition, I hope to hear soon of her convalescence. Pray give my polite remembrance to the S Hal family & Northgate. Poor Dr Hunter65 was buried on Saturday, many respectable gentlemen attended in procession, it was a solemn meeting. Poor little John Hunter was chief mourner & cried bitterly. The first Mrs Hunter's remains were taken out of a vault in the Minster & interred with the Doctor's in Belfries as specified in his will. Mrs H. bears his loss tolerably.

Mr & Mrs Duffin go into the country on Wednesday week66 so that I shall most likely remain in York that week.

Mrs Boulton has arrived at Calcutta67, I have heard of her & expect the India Fleet will soon bring me tidings from herself.

Lady Crawfurd has been in York lately I do not think it unlikely we may meet her at Scarbro! I have been no sharer in the gaieties of the winter not liking the very late hours, but I think if I live & have health next winter I shall mix a little in the busy crowd, though at any time I cannot acquire a great relish for it.

You cannot imagine how hot the weather is, I never walk in a morning from its intenseness.

Pray tell me in your next how Marian is & also if she has gone to school yet. Give my best love to her & your Sons & also kind regards to Mr Lister. –

Let me now assure you I can never cease to love you & that my best wished ever attend you. If I have ever the power of adding to your happiness believe me that power shall be exerted to the utmost. The remembrance of your kindness & the happy hours I have spent in your society steals over my heart & brightens every hour.

Indeed my melancholy position finds most pleasure in the retrospect of past days. If I write dismally excuse me for I am not very well & the thought that if all this should soon terminate in death sometimes affects my spirits.

Adieu, only assure me you will believe the affection of yr affectionate E. Raine

My love to Anne, Mr & Mrs Duffin's compliments to yrself & Mr Lister. Pray do not shew my letter to Anne, at least my sad ending, for she will scold me – but you will excuse it –

PS Miss Swann desires her love to ye S Hall family & wishes to hear from them -

Eliza's illness was unspecified and undiagnosed. On May 15th she was not only ill, but also in mourning for the recent death in York of elderly Dr Hunter who had been physician in charge of York Lunatic Asylum, and whose widow was a friend of aunt Anne.

She still sent '*epistles*' to Anne, but now her letters were shorter, twice monthly and far less ardent. Anne had grown cooler but still relied on her money, and Eliza still wanted the Listers as her family. Their relationship was now more distant even though Eliza would inherit in three years' time (unless she married).

Eliza admitted to Anne that she thought they would never live together after all. But Anne reassured her that all was well, and on the 5th of July she and her mother set off to collect Eliza from school and take her to Scarborough to see her uncle James just as they always did. However on the way back through York Anne called at the Manor School to ask about returning as a day scholar, since Eliza was about to leave.

She had stopped writing her diary but Anne encouraged her to begin again on July 7th 1809. Anne was planning to be a writer to achieve independence and was using her diary as writing practice.

Eliza's journal was much more basic but often included the same details, such as on August 5th when they both returned from Scarborough to York and stopped at Langton Hall on the way to visit Isabella Norcliffe.

In August the Listers returned to Halifax and Eliza joined Mr & Mrs Duffin at Red House. Mrs Duffin was now bed-ridden. Miss Marsh, Eliza's governess, was away; she had gone to her brother's house in Winterslow, Somerset to help her sister-in-law give birth to a first son on the 27th of July. Miss Marsh's brother had inherited the family resources and become an Anglican vicar, and her two elder sisters had become Mrs Crompton of Nunmonkton and Mrs Greenup of Halifax. She herself had no dowry so remained single, as younger siblings did, though she had been educated as a governess.

So now she lived in lodgings opposite Mr Duffin and was concerned with his upbringing of the Raine sisters. Accordingly she returned to Red House on October 3rd and encouraged Eliza to read novels and religious tracts. Her birthday was on October 18th and the Jubilee of King George III on the 25th; after that Miss Marsh left Red House to return home for the York season beginning the next day. 68

At Christmas Anne's parents went to Market Weighton to stay with Rebecca's mother, and on the way they took Anne to York to stay with Eliza and the Duffins. The two young ladies danced in the Assembly Rooms and saw Madame Catalani at the theatre.

In the middle of this Miss Marsh was again called upon to help care for her sick nephew Samuel Crompton. In her absence Anne felt privileged to be invited to spend another weekend with the Duffins; life was very good, predictable and destined never to change.

A Madame Catalani 69
Quels accous! Quelle mélodie!
Sommes nous aux concerts des dieux?
Aux transports dont l'âme est ravie
On se croit habitant des creux.

Des arts n'est-ce pas le genie
Qui montre à son peuple chère
La déesse de l'harmonie
Sous les traits de Catalani?

[To Madame Catalani!
What energy! What a melody!
Are we at the concert of the Gods?
When our spirits are transported
We are not on the earth at all.

Aren't the arts marvellous
For showing its dear friends
The goddess of harmony
In the guise of Catalani?]

1810

On 21st January Henry Boulton, based in Calcutta, bought an ensignship in the East India Company army70 and became a Captain.

In York the New Year brought in much dancing and revelry despite '*influenza*' sweeping through the city. Eliza went to Nunmonkton to avoid the virus. But it soon spread as far as Halifax, to John, the eldest of Anne's two brothers. His illness rapidly became so severe that on the fifteenth of February Captain Lister called Anne home.

Despite desperate nursing around the clock by Anne and her brother Samuel, who both stayed up with him all night in place of servants, John's condition worsened into "*inflammation of the Brain*".71 After midnight on the 24th "*his breath changed to be more deathly, so much so that I immediately felt it at my chest… He frothed a little at the mouth …which only needed wiping two or three times. Waiting some time and finding John no better we called up my father at seven minutes to 3. He got up to see the last minutes of our dear, ever to be remembered and ever to be regretted John, who died without a struggle or a groan at five minutes after 3.*

John would have been 15 the …February following."   72

It was a dreadful, unexpected shock. Throughout all fourteen years of his life John had been a happy, strong, healthy boy; but he died after just three weeks of influenza. He had been the active, intelligent heir to the whole Lister family; but now out of all four sons only quiet, timid Samuel was left.

Anne wrote the sad news to York and got a reply from Miss Marsh because Eliza had caught the 'flu' but was now recovering; she was sent a mourning pelisse and a bonnet in black. Anne also caught the flu and wore a "*blister*" of mustard powder because of her "*chest attack*"; she slept in her sister's room and tried to keep her engagements, but had to be carried back from the Alexanders in a sedan chair on the 16th of February.

Anne had lost her closest sibling so she certainly suffered the trauma of bereavement. However she had always been third in line for the Lister inheritance, and now suddenly she was second in line; this changed her social and marriage prospects considerably. She was suddenly forced to reassess what she wanted and think seriously about her own personal future.

As a mark of renaissance her rebellious adolescent behaviour ceased overnight. She suddenly became respectable and began to model her behaviour on good men she knew. Her diaries, to date written on scraps of paper and leftover notebooks, now became important for introspection and analysis. She started to use dated exercise books as diaries, and indexed them properly.

Eliza left school that Christmas, so it was time for Anne to return. She asked Mr Duffin if she could have Eliza's room; he said yes. That meant Eliza had to find her own address, but it was not difficult. She had no qualms about living with Lady Crawfurd, despite her sister's difficulties, because she had a softer, more rational personality. In any case it was only for a few years. In a new diary on 5th April 1810 she wrote that she was looking forward to the future. She was leaving York and the Duffin family "*forever*" in order to share "*Housekeeping*" with her cousin until Anne had finished studying, when they would live together in Halifax. Anne accompanied her by coach as far as Ferrybridge as she left the city and made her way to her new address at Mrs Turnbull's lodgings, Hallgate, Doncaster.

Lady Mary Crawfurd's mother had been William Raine's sister. When her father died Mary was his sole heir, so she had a good dowry. On 11th August 1793 she had married Robert Crawfurd, an army captain, heir to Sir Robert Crawfurd of Pollok Castle, Renfrew, Scotland. In 1794 he succeeded to the title and bought promotion. Nevertheless his wife divorced him six years later because he turned out to be homosexual. 73

She received £130 a year in settlement; not enough for an upper-class life. However William Raine's legacy of £170 per annum gave her the £300 she needed. She was also his trustee, so she felt she should act as guardian to her nieces. She was 35 years older, their appearance wa disconcerting and they were bastards, but it was her duty to marry them off as soon as possible. Jane was now married and off her hands, but her sister seemed easier to deal with.

Eliza had troubles from the start.

Miss Lister, Micklegate, York74

My dear Lister

Mrs Waterton's maid having unexpectedly called upon Lady Crawfurd I cannot let her go without giving my friend a line. She will tell you I am well & looking so too I expect. I understand from a letter to Lady C. from Mrs Bindlass there is a letter from India which we expect tomorrow my heart misgives me at the name of India for long that be a painful subject & why & wherefore Lady C. should receive a letter from India annoys me -- Is it do you think an account of Jane's death though ye release would be perhaps a blessing yet I should grieve over it as if I had doated on her & sustained a heavy loss –

Tell Mr & Mrs Duffin I am always thinking of them. Many a pleasure long gone by ye remembrance of which casts sometimes a melancholy over my mind but I ought to be happy Lady C. is kind to me beyond expression & my days are as peaceful as I could wish yet I cannot forget you all my darling friend a loss incomparable indeed I have always loved you better than I ever could my unfortunate Sister.

But I must not forget the disappointment we have received this morning ye people Mrs Postlethwaite is with won't let her come to me are therefore destitute of a Servant & Lady C. made me write ys morning to Mrs Hurst to look out for one immediately for us. We are not very much inconvenienced having met with a clever charwoman – you must come to us soon Lady C. won't be refused.

Adieu dear L. I have not time to add more than that I am your … E.R best love to all

Lady C. desires the best regards. Best love to Miss M. do tell me when you are going to leave York & don't forget to write to me by Tuesday.

Again adieu my dear L. & believe me you are forever in ye remembrance of your friend.

The anticipated letter from India was to say that after twenty-two months of marriage Jane was returning home. She had been abandoned by her husband after his promotion and was obliged to throw herself on the mercy of her friends and her sister.

The news did not have a good effect on Lady Crawfurd. On April 15th Eliza wrote to Anne that her cousin had been "*taken ill*", on the 17th she was "*fractious*", and the next day that she was "*unmanageable*". Three days later they two women had an "*altercation*" so that Lady Crawfurd was "*very cross*" and they were no longer on speaking terms.

Miss Lister, Willm Duffins Esqr. Micklegate York   April 15
 75

My dear L. will be somewhat surprised to see a letter from me so soon again but the reason of my writing is that having a parcel to send to York I cannot resent the pleasure I must ever feel in scribbling a few lines to you.

The occasion is melancholy, but such I have often experienced in a varied degree. My heart seems unusually oppressed & overwhelmed with hope & fear. My sister is I suspect again in England and is perhaps now busying herself with hopes of that happiness which a kind reception from her friends might afford. Now, she may flatter herself, is an end to my once and past pains, but Lister how disappointed will she be? I fear the consequences.

I wish you would speak to Mr Duffin yourself and beg him not to be sudden in the disclosure of his suspicions & sentiments regarding her. Yet I cannot help thinking her innocent. She is a peculiar character & must be accordingly judged of & treated & what might wear the appearance of criminal conduct in another may be in her quite the contrary. She has always acted without reason & I wish that in this affair & at this moment she could be excused of having acted so.

Yesterday Lady C. got a letter from Jane which you will read.

Today one has arrived from Mr Parkins76 not written by himself I think but with his signature subjoined, expressing himself feelingly enough. From his orthography I at first thought he must be very ignorant, but on comparing the 2 handwritings I supposed he might not be deserving of my accusation as the writing that letter might have devolved on one of his clerks.

I have written to Mr Duffin & you will deliver his letter & those for India immediately. I think there must be letters also for me, which we agreed ere I left York should be opened for Mrs Duffin's use.

Lady C. is this morning violently ill in a headache but as these are occasional things I am not alarmed & firmly believe tomorrow will see her quite well; she has a delicate habit & much injured from various causes, but with great care she may live many years, perhaps live to see many inferior in age drop into ye grave - she is extremely good to me, I think her attachment to me very great & I hope I shall always make her feel comfortable & happy.

Amidst all my present enjoyments I never forget York nor its past delightful pleasures & fully opined am I that there is an unspeakable charm in ye retrospection of our earlier years at York. I was at school at York I received my education & was happy under my guardian's roof, no wonder then I love it very much indeed and my dear Lister I shall long remember it –

I expect you are all gaiety don't do too much though for you are very delicate – I don't expect that in York you will find much leisure to write to me long letters as long as you are [-] I think me worthy of your attachment & kindness – your brief epistles will make me perfectly happy & content.

According to your desire I wrote to Miss Swann & had meant to have done ye same to good Mrs Swann yesterday but something unforeseen prevented me & now I feel I must put it off altogether till I am more at ease.

Pray don't forget to communicate every thing concerning Mrs Boulton & all Mr Duffin's intentions of course. I must be very anxious till she is settled in some place as Mr Duffin could wish. You will be surprised to find Mrs Boulton has been a prisoner in ye isle of France.

If you would wish my dear friend to delay your next letter to me thinking you may have something more to add interesting to me I will not feel disappointed.

I can now my dear L. pronounce myself quite convalescent my cough entirely gone & my good looks returned. Had ye day been fine I should have walked out. I have cast off my shawl & all my unnecessary wrappings I am taking asses' milk in a morning.

You have received my note I hope by Mrs Waterton's Servant which would inform you of our disappointment respecting Mrs Postlethwaite's we are not very awkwardly situated having got a good clever woman into ye house –I hope Mrs Hunt will be able to get us one that will be suitable.

Excuse my sad ~~scribb~~ scrawl I have not many moments to devote to you. May this find you all well & I am sure you happy I suppose you sometimes think of me & kindly wish me every good –

I am at times dull for want of your society Lady C. & I read & talk & work but the affectionate manners of my friend are often wanting to complete my happiness. As I have sent you 2 intervening letters before my usual day for writing I won't promise to write again till next Friday or Saturday when I can send you an epistle more intelligible than this. God bless you & give you every happiness & Believe me dear L. Yours truly affectionate   E.R.

I send this parcel to you thinking it better for you to receive it & defray it - do not be later with your letter to me than Wednesday –

P.S. you can bring the India letters with you when you determine to visit us –…

Jane's "*criminal conduct*" was pregnancy, and not by her husband. Eliza's last letter to Anne had been blotched with tears; in this one she was in a hurry and constantly crossing out her words. She was also very anxious about not receiving any news about her sister.

April 21st Doncaster Saturday 3 o'clock

As we don't dine till 4 I have just an hour my dear Lister to devote to you after being out ye whole morning – It is now 5 days since the usual time for my hearing from you I have felt greatly & deeply disappointed at your forgetfulness of me & now am fearful there is some alarming cause for such unusual negligence from you therefore dear Lister if you have any consideration for my feelings answer me by return of post tell me why I am thus forgotten at a time so interesting.

If you are ill any kind friend would write for you & if you are well I can hardly forgive you for your inattention – I have day after day excused you to myself as I know I gave you a day or two beyond Tuesday thinking you might have more to communicate respecting my unfortunate Sister but at last Saturday has arrived & I am still ignorant of Mr Duffin's determinations or whether you received my first long letter my note by Mrs Waterton's maid or the parcel I sent you last Sunday enclosing 2 letters for Lady C. from Mr Parkins & Jane.

I only beg an answer by return of post to ease my sufferings I do feel severely for during our long intimacy & attachment I never have yet once had to upbraid you for this fault I do not impute it to want of regard for me this would be injustice to you & me, but I fear it is indisposition or some other serious cause & if you are ill & neglect acquainting me with it how can I forgive you Never do so again I entrust of you dear L. you know the weakness of my nature its rooted imbecility & if you can love me still you will not add another pang to my heart. If you can't write may I beg Miss Marsh will take ye trouble & oblige me – Now I cannot scold you more I have said enough & shall now wait anxiously for Monday morning may it make me happier how ill could I now hear multiplied disappointment or painful intelligence of your illness –

My health is thank God excellent I got out last Monday & have been out every day since –

Lady Crawfurd & I have even had a serious altercation her temper is unaltered has after all a good heart good intentions & affection for me …[illegible] … an unpleasant fractiousness –

this morning Sarah Mrs Duffin's maid called on me I was delighted to see any one that had been the member of Mr Duffin's family, I delight I remembrance of this kind Tell Mr & Mrs D I often think of them & that I hope Mrs D will in future remind you to write to me has York my dear friend banished me from your recollection I cannot believe it Nothing I hope will make you careless of giving me pleasure, you can little know what pain you have given me.

Mrs Hurst has procured us a Servant who lived with Mrs George Lloyd as housemaid we expect her on Tuesday. On that day some young people dine with us from the Schools amongst them little Woolley of the Grange.

Mrs Willis of Badsworth invited us to spend a few nights next Week during her Son's day but that we have refused as leaving Doncaster at present would be ridiculous & unpleasant.

Every day I have sent to the Hotels or Inns for parcels supposing you might send me one but all has been fruitless & joyless! But I told you I would have done with this subject & I will for tho my mood is an angry & painful one yet when I remember Lister I cannot but feel more of affection & forgiveness than displeasure. Already a fortnight has elapsed since leaving York neither weeks nor years can deprive me of solicitude for you –

If I err or offend in this freedom of epistolary converse excuse me I am compelled by many a sentiment many a nameless suffering –

Give to Mr & Mrs Duffin my best love & most affectionate wishes to Miss M, & other friends kind remembrances –

To yourself my dear, but naughty friend the best sensations of a grateful & long attached heart which knows full well how to appreciate its early & kindest companion –

It is late now some interruptions make it impossible to fill my sheet adieu if you want to hear from me – I'll write again next week but if not you need not expect an epistle till Friday or Saturday.

Lady C. is making preparations for your promised visit don't be alarmed at ye word preparations they are not formal ones. Again farewell & believe me dear L. Yours truly affectionate E.R.

But Anne had been writing regularly. Within a week Eliza realised that Lady Crawfurd was hiding her letters from Anne, turning down invitations and rejecting social involvements without telling her about them. This included urgent news about her sister.

Jane had suffered a traumatic journey home, as a dark-skinned young woman alone, unguarded and unchaperoned on board a ship full of men for six months. When she finally disembarked in France she had been thrown into prison until she could prove British nationality. Here she had either been raped or had bought what she needed with her only asset. Exhausted, pregnant, distressed and with no more than the clothes she stood up in, Jane had at last made it to London. First she sought help from Mr James of Coutts Bank, who had dealt with her affairs in the past, then she went to see Mr Duffin in York.

But Duffin could not give her money; she had given all hers away. Nor could he treat her as his ward; she wasn't Raine any more, she was now Boulton, so Eliza was not able to help her either. On the other hand in 1810 it was a criminal act for a wife to have another man's baby, and a plea of rape was no defence, so she dared not go to the Boultons. They would support their son and send her to prison.

Financially Eliza was currently protected because Duffin held her money in trust while she was under 21, but after this her position would be difficult. She did her best to follow advice and abandon Jane and her child, ignore her sister and coming niece or nephew. However they were both bereft of their parents and home, and had promised to help each other.

Mr Duffin had always been their guardian, but now he had abandoned Jane and was making Eliza live with Lady Crawfurd so that Anne could take her place. Did he prefer Anne because she was white? Eliza was still in love with her 'husband' but now Anne was much less loyal or approachable. Eliza couldn't talk to anyone in case it made the whole situation worse; it was socially unmentionable. All she could do was allow her husband freedom; Anne's passions might be over as soon as they had begun.

Eliza wrote to Anne requesting that Mr Duffin should be kind to Jane when giving the "bad news" that she could not expect any help from him. Jane was no longer a gentlewoman like her sister; she was now a penniless "fallen" woman with an illegitimate child and she no longer had the means to keep her offspring. She would have to go to the workhouse and work for her living.77 Nevertheless Duffin found her lodgings while she was pregnant, at Fulford in the less salubrious part of the city.

Miss Lister Mr & Mrs Duffin's Esqr Micklegate York

1810 Doncaster Sunday noon after church April 22.   ¼ to 2 o'clock

My dear, dear Lister

What happiness do I experience from the long looked for epistle from one of my best & dearest of friends Oh Lister little can you conceive what a burden my heart is rid of.

But amidst all my joy I cannot help being very seriously alarmed at ye fate of those letters I have written to you & that from yourself to me which it seems we have neither of us seen & are ignorant of until this mutual & I trust happy disclosure. My dear L. how painfully I have thought of you many days, have endured a tormenting solicitude. Illness I feared was the cause of your silence but thank God your health is unimpaired & that the mistakes & errors originated solely in those who have had the management of the parcels & letters.

That you may be able to know what to expect from the post office I must tell you that on Wednesday ye 10th I wrote you a long letter on a long sheet. On Friday I gave Mrs Waterton's maid a note for you which would speak of this letter. On Sunday I enclosed a letter from Mr Parkins & one from Mrs Boulton from Calcutta to Lady C., in a parcel to Mr Duffin to whom also I wrote & sent a letter to yourself in it, which parcel I directed to you also & sent it by the Royal Charlotte Post Coach which leaves Doncaster for ye North at 3 o'clock in ye afternoon, to the Proprietor of which last Coach I sent this morning & who this day has written himself to York as it was booked to enquire concerning it –

I am unconscious what letters you have written to me I have only received your first dated Monday ye 9th & your last this morning you see now completely ye whole affair. –

But allow me to say dear L. how happy I feel at hearing from you & particularly at a time when every feeling of mine is naturally in agitation.

Poor Jane is she really abandoned & impenitent! To say much on this subject is useless & become now joyless, hopeless. I hear it my friend I hope as I ought. Time will reconcile me to its afflicting nature; rely on my bearing it with resignation.

I have many, many pleasures left my friends are kind & sincere I have more blessings than I deserve. Thank Mr Duffin & Mrs Duffin for all their goodness & the trouble they have had & still have for this unfortunate Sister & beg of them also to offer my gratitude to Mr James for ye immense trouble he is taking upon himself to soften the situation of an undeserving object. I think I should at the conclusion of this affair return Mr James my thanks for such goodness.

No doubt you have letters to me from Jane & much you have to tell me too but dear Lister if those letters are very distressing burn them & let me not have the pain of reading them. My heart is now very full though I was prepared for the subject you will forgive me my dear friend – this is the weakness of human nature –

Lady Crawfurd desires her best love to you & feels inexpressibly shocked at the unavoidable appearance she must make to you & hopes you will now see any intentional neglect could not possibly have been meant towards you to whom she has been longing to write ever since I came but has been unwell & harassed with many unforeseen occurrences& which she wished to have done when we were settled with a servant feeling then more at liberty to say she was ready & wishful to receive you as a visitor.

I was indeed much shocked at your account of Mrs Wall's death I knew & liked her & pity the surviving husband whose affliction must be great.

Tomorrow I am in hope I shall have an answer to my letter written yesterday & I require from you dear L. another letter on receiving this I am anxious to know how & why this chain of errors & mistakes occur. You are well I hope this you must tell me particularly. My next will be a longer letter than this I shall then be collected & tranquil at present therefore I can say little else than what immediately concerns the present moment.

Allow me to say we hope to see you at your promised time. Lady C. expects you will now particularly give proof of you kindness to me by coming & consoling me & indeed talking over the events that have taken place since I left York – I have many commissions to give you before that & much to say therefore several letters will be exchanged between us.

We have just left church which seldom is over before 1 o'clock. We talk of going again I cannot say more.

Adieu my very dear friend & believe me most Affectionately Yours E.R.

Say what you think best to every friend of mine.

Eliza had felt herself pulled in different directions by everyone around her. Anxious about her sister and increasingly nervous about her cousin, Eliza demanded that Anne visit her in Doncaster, but Lady Crawfurd declined at first, unwilling to let strangers disturb her routine. Anyway Eliza's regular attendance at church should calm her down.

Then on the 24th of April another parcel sent from York to Doncaster had gone missing. And within the next two weeks Lady Crawfurd had arbitrarily taken over all responsibility for household and finances, ignoring their previous agreement. To top it all, despite Eliza's wishes, she had invited a suitor, Mr Willis, to tea.

Wednesday morng. Doncaster April 25th 181078

Dear Lister

You will I presume expect a line from me in my parcel to Mrs Swann to whom I mean to write today.

This morning our Servant has arrived & Lady C. is busying herself in giving her her regulations. This Betty Johnson who last served as housemaid at Mrs G Lloyd's is an unpolished Yorkshire looking lass extremely desirous apparently to oblige & suit us. She is not acquainted with Cooking however our good Mrs Turnbull is to instruct her until she is more knowing in ye Art & God grant we may all now go on peaceably & happily –

You may now expect to hear from Lady C. with her long intended invite; come to us dear L., I have set my heart upon having you & you well know how ill I can bear disappointment; at this time too an inward something asks it; you can talk over ye late sad subject with me, teach me calm submission & elevate those dark despairing feelings which sometimes break upon my enjoyment. But dear L, in ye interim write me more fully about yourself & my other friends.

My Cold is no worse & I expect ye warm weather will rid me of it.

Lady C has just finished ye Novel lent us by Mrs Willis called Zofloya or ye Moor written by P. Dacre. I hate Novels & Romances. I hope this sort of reading will not long continue.

Of my parcel I begin to have fears, yesterday we called at the office with enquiries about it, ye Bookkeeper appeared drunk but said he would use his exertions to have it found.

As I never hide anything from you I will not disguise that I am not always very comfortable with my relative but this I think will die away when I have become more familiar with her conduct; if you reprove me for allowing myself to be so you will make me very unhappy for I always endure ye most painful sorrow when under you displeasure –

Remember dear Lister mine is become a peculiar situation I feel orphan like & unprotected in the society of Lady C, she is a Child & sometimes a tyrant in action but my trust is in that last & forever remaining consolation my Religion & my God may he protect me –

By my strain you will say I am melancholy but I don't feel so & I am unwilling to alter my situation or my companion. God bless you Lister you can I know remember with pleasure

Your Affectionate E.R.

Best love to my dear Mrs D … You'll write won't you when I asked you? I shall feel very grateful for your compliance once more adieu my beloved friend –

Eliza began to feel "*very dejected*".79 Anne's next letter to her was smuggled inside a parcel from their friend Mrs Swann; but the missing parcel was elusive.

Three days later during another quarrel Eliza was told "*intelligence of £100 allowed to Lady C*", paid annually by Mr Duffin out of Eliza's own trust fund. This put their whole relationship into a different light: Lady C was being paid a considerable sum to accommodate her. Was she being treated as an item for sale? Was no family feeling involved? Enraged, Eliza demanded again that Anne be allowed to visit, and this time there was no refusal; she arrived in Doncaster on 30th April.

Doncaster May 10th 1810 near 11 morning   80

My dear Lister

Your anxiously looked for letter arrived ys morning whilst I was dressing. Its contents pleased & soothed my heart which fills with gratitude to Mr Duffin for his indulgent acquiescence to my wishes & his kind interest in my happiness.

After you left me my dear friend I felt destitute of every present comfort yet I was not so selfish as to forget to rejoice at your escape from so much misery which so unfortunately seemed portioned out for you to bear during your short visit at Doncaster you left me to be much happier amongst ye best & kindest of friends where I am glad you arrived safe & well.

Never have I shed one tear until this moment the contemplation of better days has hitherto kept up my spirits but sometimes even this cannot remove ye heaviness of present disappointment.

I shall write to Mr Duffin in a day or two and disclose my whole heart to him at present perhaps I am not quite composed enough to write as I could wish I have no doubt of his permitting me to engage in those plans you have so kindly suggested to me.

After Mr & Mrs Duffin you are well aware I have no nearer or dearer tie than yourself; and as my Sister's unfortunate conduct at once annihilates my desire to fix near York it is natural & reasonable I think that my wishes should lead me to reside as near you as possible & this Mr Duffin will plainly see –

Your enquiries about my health I can answer quite to your satisfaction I am now perfectly well no more tendency to cough nor any other bodily symptom of pain. The day you left me I had a bad headache which obliged me to retire early; the next day I had a severe bowel complaint when I was compelled again to find relief in my

bed where I lay till ye evening & then got up much better. This morning I am as well as ever I was in my life & ye return of warm weather induces me to walk in my favourite garden today where you & I have spent many a pleasant hour –

Surprised indeed must Mr & Mrs Duffin be at Lady Crawfurd's conduct to you; you who never gave offence or provocation to a mortal being in your life that accusation believe me dear L. has given me more pain than all ye accumulation of insults & ungovernable rage directed to myself during ye whole of that time I have spent with her –

since your departure Lady C has scarcely uttered therefore we have had little opportunity of conversing, her health is quite restored her voice also, the loss of which Mr Shepherd imported to her nervousness alone, she has never mentioned you for whom I have no doubt she feels a great aversion. How long her taciturnity will remain I cannot have an idea however it is far preferable than an eternal fractiousness and I wish it may continue for my peace of mind –

I beg you will write to me by next Tuesday before which time I shall have written to Mr Duffin & you will then tell me perhaps when your Father & Mother return & when Mr & Mrs Duffin leave York for Red House –

I have few pleasures but your letters all other inferior ones now seem unsubstantial & transient therefore my dear friend will not omit her usual punctuality in writing them -

My chief thoughts shall be as you desired employed in benefitting my health, which I am sure will soon be reinstated my mind at ease & then my health is at ease too –

You desired me to look for a paper which had an account of your expences I have searched every drawer & cannot find it therefore it must be in yr box perhaps enclosed in one of your letters.

I am very sorry to hear of Mrs Duffin's cold how very delicate she is I really thought ye fine mild weather would have sheltered her from all attack of cold pray give my kind love to her & wishes for her restoration which will be permanent I daresay when she goes to Red House. I suppose you have said so much to Mr Duffin concerning me that there is little left for me to say than a repetition of ye whole which I think I ought myself to make known.

How thankful I am to hear of my poor Sister's comfortable abode depraved as she has been I still feel very great pity for her she has never had sense or understanding to shield her from temptation for to whom little is given much cannot be expected, I hope after her confinement she will lead a better life & reform but I have many a fear she could nor never can I think withstand temptation. –

How good has Mr Duffin been I feel I can never repay the debt of obligation I owe to my excellent Guardian perhaps dear Lister & as we have often thought the day may come when I can at least offer more substantial proof of gratitude than mere words – say to Mr Duffin all you know I feel at this present moment for sure he is a friend to the fatherless & needy, often my Sister & I have found him so.

Take great care of yourself dear Lister thankful I am to hear of your good health long may it continue to comfort all those many friends which your goodness & amiable disposition have gained –

The weeks that are destined me to pass here with Lady C I shall employ as well as I can, improvements of different denominations & when you next meet me you expect to find me … better I hope in knowledge. No progress have I made of long in those studies which I daily feel are necessary to ye completion of an enlightened mind & if I let my years now pass away in idleness & inactivity it will soon be too late to recall them & soon too late to endeavour at perfection –

When I am more under your immediate eye I shall hope to gain much & to have my hours better regulated what real happiness do I anticipate from your society & kindness I only fear after so much disappointment ye quick succession of calm & contented enjoyment will too greatly elate my weak helpless heart –

I ask of you dear Lister to teach me to properly estimate my blessings & to inculcate those principles which are ye basis of a virtuous character then may I not be unworthy [of] those friends which God has granted me –

You told me that you have shewn some of my former letters to Mr & Mrs Duffin let me hope you will not submit this to their inspection for I should never write with confidence or freedom if I knew you did it – adieu my dear friend with my best & most affectionate remembrance to Mr & Mrs D & Miss Marsh Believe me your sincerely attached E.R.

P.S. I have opened my letter again for ye purpose of informing you that Lady C is so past bearing that I am resolved to write ys day & post Mr D & beg leave to have matters as speedily determined as possible & then surely Lady C will cease to torment me. Adieu

Doncaster May 18. Friday morng aft. 981

When there was a delay of 2 days I did begin to think my dear Friend had not forgotten me but neglected me however I judged ye motive to be what it was & readily excused you to my very much attached heart. I am glad you are so happy so gay & so cheerful & I hope you may long be so.

I was a little checked not dejected at your information concerning Miss Mellin's [postponement of accommodation] in my sanguine hopes of happiness. You have been very kind in writing to me & we must now look forward with hope; I do, & glad shall I be when I am at liberty. You won't be surprised that I count ye weeks, nay even days to my looked for emancipation & every night God knows I thank him for ye day that is past.

To Mr Duffin's letter to Lady C I owe my present composure of mind, Lady C has ever since been moderate & peaceful. I do not feel that constant necessity for watching her looks & dreading what she next uttered as fearing my life depend upon it, you now know my situation & that I can very well bear ye allotted few weeks for my continuance here.

On Wednesday morng Lady C feeling herself more able for ye exertion requested of me ye cause of my (as she terms it) strange basehearted conduct. I gave her ye reasons for my conduct & informed her of my determination & ye misery which I endured from her bad temper. In answer to this I was told she considered me a very degraded mortal *indeed & gave me such abuse as I would not have taken from any one else whom I expected were talking in their senses however my dear L. when we meet I will relate to you ye whole of our conversation suffice it for ye present to say she gave me her curse & told me that the heavy vengeance of heaven would fall upon me sooner or later for my basehearted irrational conduct to her, devoid also of duty & affection & added to this I must tell you she suspects you & I have been acting together in some deep plot against her to injure her.*

During ye whole of our conversation I endeavoured to preserve an unruffled temper but I will not but allow I secretly felt my pride wounded my good intentions trampled upon & myself insulted –

I find she has rejected ye £100 per annum so generously offered by Mr D for my sake at least request of Mr Duffin to restore it & to put into execution his first intention –

Lady C has written to Mr D & at ye conclusion of her ye other day's not peace offerings she said to me, it was her desire none but those already acquainted with ye cause of my leaving her should know ye real cause; & that she begged I would report some family pecuniary occurrence was ye reason of this sudden separation. To this I agreed so warn my good friends dear L., & in future do you not reveal ye real affair & ye motives for it; Lady C also requested we might appear as cordial as ever; visit together walk together etc. as she would not like a contrary proceeding does not this sound like a consciousness of error Lister?

Poor Lady Crawfurd amidst all I pity her very very much what a misfortune it is to have so uncontrollable a temper I wish her happiness I wish her friends & may God give them her. I will never desert her, though I will never live with her. Enough has now been said on a subject that has cost me much I will drop it & endeavour to forget it. –

I pass my time as well as I can, I read, work, walk, play & vary my employments, my health is considerably better & I even think I am getting fat.

Good Mrs Percival Sister to Mr Whitaker I met last week, from her I have a most warm invitation to spend my leisure moments there she observed me melancholy, as I was, & distantly hinted at ye true cause having been witness of my Sister's return from Pomfret. When she knows ye whole business I mean tomorrow to sit half an hour there but I shall strictly adhere to the promise I have made Lady C.

I hope your Symphitum Asperiamum arrived safe I expect you would get it about 4 o'clock yesterday. I myself saw it packed up, chose ye best looking plant & gave it into ye Guard's hands, who promised to put it into his pocket & not fail to deliver it safely into Micklegate – It was 2 shillings, & ye Lupin tree eighteen pence.

My old friend ye Gardener is so civil to me he makes me feel quite attached to him, I endeavour not to wear ye appearance of dejection & yet ye old man often comes after me & makes some pretext to engage me in conversation & then concludes with saying "why Miss you must excuse my boldness but you look so grave so I came to talk to you

& pray come into my Greenhouse that I may amuse you", this pleases me very much Lister & then I say to myself I am not quite destitute of pleasure & a well meaning companion –

I received a most kind letter from Miss Swann on Tuesday whose good counsels I shall adopt as being ye most friendly to assuage present unhappiness. I believe her a sincere friend & as such I greatly value her, give her my best regards & say I will not write to her until you leave York as you will tell her all about me for ye present.

I am delighted to hear you have got so pleasant a companion as Miss Norcliffe.82 I never doubted of your making friends wherever you went & I hope long to have ye opportunity of congratulating you upon it; but amidst all your happiness & pleasure dear Lister you forget to answer me 2 or 3 questions I asked you in my last, say a little more about yourself I am very anxious to know what you mean to do.

The return of mild weather again I hope will make Mrs Duffin better tell her so with my affectionate love. By Mr D's letter to me I suppose they go to Red House in a week. Is your intention ye same as when I saw you to refute ye pleasure of accompanying then into the country?

Lady C is well I believe but does not yet rise to breakfast nor till 11 or 12.

The Strafforth & Tichhill Local Militia have now succeeded ye Staincross.

I would give you an outline of the History of England I am reading but I fear I better defer all ys till we meet you not having leisure to attend to it. Your approbation of my letter to Mr D very much delights me because I always fancy you think & know well. My cloths are all prepared I have nothing to do but to read & this day 6 weeks I expect I shall depart.

Anxiously shall I wish ye arrival of Miss Mellin's letter; thus far I have learnt in my sojourn in life not to be too sanguine in my expectations & to remember thorns are scattered in our way to ye attainment of earthly happiness; the God I profess is greater than ye evil allotted me therefore I am not as yet very much better off than millions.

Let me beg of you dear L to write to me regularly & never to put off my pleasure but on some very momentous occasion. I said before I have no other pleasure & at a time like this a long letter & regular writing of them appear greater comfort than ends83 tell me if you can what are ye plans of entering Miss Mellin's abode etc. etc. & I am certain when you hear from her you will not delay a moment acquaintg me with it - & not till ye beginning of June must I expect ye decision. I am afraid you forget your own concerns by never mentiong that you have to enquire about Johnson's niece at Mrs Wilson's.

Have you heard from your Mother? & have you ordered my shoes at Hornby? I do not wonder at yr becoming a member of ye friendly society for I have long ceased to wonder.

Remember me to all who enquire after me as you think I ought to mention them. To Mr & Mrs Duffin & Miss Marsh my best remembrance; ask Mr Duffin if in the beginning of June there be fine warm weather I may cast off my pelisse84 & put on my summer habiliments. I have left off fires & gradually endeavour to get hardy. You will laugh when I tell you that for a whole week Mr Duffin's letter to me was ye first thing I read immediately on awakening consequently you may suppose it lay under my pillow every night. This act seemed very rational to me at the time but now I can't help acknowledging ye babiness of ye trick so don't oppose me it only shews what a comfort it was to me -----

I sent ye plant by ye Lord Neeson85 -

Adieu my dear Lister thro' life you will always find how gratefully my heart acknowledges your distinguished & most estimable friendship yours affectionately E.R.

Doncaster May 23d 1810   Wednesday morng 10 o'clock86

My dear Lister,

The receipt of your last letter has given me unusual pleasure but I am sorry very sorry I assure you to have said anything that you were not deserving of; perhaps when my mind was harassed by so many painful events I might have inadvertently written harshly to you but if I have & you have felt it you must forgive me when I tell you I feel I can never intentionally offend you & that if I knew I had done it I should know no peace until; I had made amends. You are my dear & long tried friend I am attached to you as to a parent & without you dear L. I am helpless & unhappy. All this you know & therefore need not a repetition only forgive me & I am satisfied.

I am at present writing in my bedroom finding it impossible downstairs as Lady C is constantly interrupting me.

On Monday last she repeated one of her trying conversations & demanded from me a greater respect & humility towards her Ladyship in short talked so imperiously that I dreaded ye consequence, however all is hushed again & I live tolerably at peace I exert myself to amuse her & according to her request in company use every deceit & speciousness, but 'tis well there is to be an end to all this soon, for I feel my spirits sometimes so broken I don't know whether life or death more desirable; but Lister Sorrow is not new to me, & I have learnt the way to divert it; time passes away & may I at last enjoy quiet & tranquillity; your letters have ye most powerful effect upon [me], they make me very happy, & when I am apt to relapse into my former dejection they recall to my mind ye necessity of exertion & teach me to value those good friends I have & which now prove so powerfully soothing to my feelings oh Lister when I remember Mr Duffin's kindness human tenderness to me at a time so exceedingly painful I shed tears of gratitude & affection thank him dear L for his additional goodness tell him that I see with him ye propriety of finishing my quarter here & that I am resolved to follow his judgment until as I said before I am compelled to quit my cousin from some furious outrage. Say this & more my dear friend you know what I feel for too much cannot be said to Mr Duffin.

I anxiously wish for Miss Mellin's letter in about a week I shall look for it, if she cannot accommodate me what is to become of me; but as to this I depend & rely upon Mr Duffin & yourself to procure me another situation.

To say I flatter myself concerning Miss Mellin would be false, for I do not, I have been so often disappointed in my hopes that I think I am not to be so helped. I would read to amuse myself but this I can hardly do if I submit to Lady C's desires; this morning Lady C receives a letter from Miss Swann which seems to have made her thoughtful. Shocked you would be I am sure dear L at Lady C's horrible imprecation; much more will shock you which I reserve for our meeting. Her health is quite good she eats drinks & walks as lithely as I do.

I have called upon Mrs Percival with whom I spent a pleasant hour she begs her kind compts to Mr & Mrs Duffin – we are acquainted also with a Miss Robson & a Mrs Judson with both of whom we pass several hours this is agreable enough. Upon reflection I think with yourself how inconsistent it is in Lady C, deserving such a reason to be alleged for our separation & I fear I must sometimes deviate in part from my promise however I can do my utmost to oblige her & she cannot expect more.

Believe me dear Lister amidst all ye gloom that pervades in my solitary heart I still can participate in your pleasures. I am truly delighted you are so happy & that you are going to Red House well may you call York a paradise with so many blessings around you, few things please me so much as your being a favorite with Mr & Mrs Duffin it is a compliment of approval to my choice independant of your merits – they know you are good & amiable & appreciate you accordingly.

When you write to your Mother give her my kind remembrance. Weighton must have charms to detain her till July however it is to hoped ye change will be beneficial to both yr Father & Mother's spirits. Little Marian leads a fine life how will all this interference with School, reconcile her to it again.

Johnson is rather annoyed at yr havg mentioned her niece to Mrs Wilson & is afraid she has made you feel awkward. She says that of course this will extract her niece's intention from her to Mrs Wilson & give you an opportunity of havg her call upon you & enquire what place she wants to undertake. In another letter I will tell you more satisfactorily about her.

Ask Mr Duffin if he will approve my leaving off my pelisse in June you forgot in yr last – I am sorry Mrs Duffin's cold is so obstinate I sincerely hope ye country air will remove it. I shall think of you all on Tuesday next you will like Red House I think very much a summer residence it is very pleasant. Thank Miss Marsh for her kind message to me & tell her how gratified I am at so many proofs of goodness give my best love to her & every wish for her happiness - & that I hope they are all well at Winterslow –

After receiving Miss Mellin's determination I shall write to my few correspondents informg them of the change in my situation & then I must thank you to send me Miss Pereira's letter –

I smile at yr particularity in yr shoes all this is vastly pleasing to me you are so metamorphosed I shall hardly know you again –

What gratitude you are to York for York has occasioned your improvements. Now you may flatter yourself dear L you are very handsome tho once you believed yourself ye most ordinary mortal being –

Pray give my very kind love to Harcourt who is so great a favorite tell him tho I have never mentioned him I have often remembered him.

To Mr & Mrs Duffin every best & affectionate love & do not omit my gratitude for his last kind message.

To Miss Swann also remember me most kindly. & Believe me dear Lister that for your sake I will use every means of making myself comfortable & happy & that I may soon see you soon enjoy a tranquil happiness.

I remain your sincerely attached E.R. my dear

Eliza was very excited about the prospect of leaving Lady Crawfurd and moving to Halifax.

*Thursday May 24. 1810*87   *Saturday morning 10 o'clock*   88

This moment I received your letter unexpected I assure you, little did I imagine your compliance would have been so early – I had just completed the scribbling of 3 letters one to Mrs D, Miss M, & Miss Swann when it arrived - & now it is justly your turn to look for my attention –

In your letter dearest Lister I see every thing that can please excepting that I want you to say the very statement good or bad of your health, I want to hear whether your cough is gone, your sleep fully returned, & whether you can tempt all weathers – These are the proofs of your entire recovery of vigour & of health

You must be mum but I find yr Father is resolving to give notice by June, that you may go into Devonshire by September - A sweet village a little to the West of Exeter is I believe in contemplation as likely to suit yr family – This has transpired without leave & if you mention it I am undone –

Ever in hurry am I, I can scarcely perform all the necessities of today. I dine early & at ¼ past 4 set off to Crownest – yesterday Evening I drank tea & supped at yr

Father's, where I spent a most agreeable Evening – yr Father is teaching the young ones amongst whom I include myself Quadrille – I am an apter scholar than I looked for -

51

& today I was asked to dinner & to dress there but have refused on the account of having more time to devote to you my very dear Friend-

Whilst I think of it Monday let me say I visit Mrs Veitch, Tuesday there is to be a party at S. Hall89, & Wednesday I prepare having some Friends, myself, Mrs Gervaise Alexander, Veitchs, Wigglesworths & all yr Families, yr Mother & Marian dine here on a joint of meat –

I have promised yr Mother to be very kind to her during the absence of her dearly beloved, for I assure you she begins already to be low about it –

The Bramleys90 are exactly as I last represented them to you excepting that poor Miss Bramley is not so well owing I daresay to grief of mind & she is now arrived at an age to feel to the full extent of this aggravated misfortune –

Dr Disney A. has commenced the Lover & is shortly to be really united to Miss Edwards of the Temple of the Wind, her jointure is I daresay very acceptable & she has kindly consented - you'll laugh at this but it is not without every proof of truth; she herself has acknowledged it & surely from such a quarter who can doubt it –

Then it is decided that the Bramley's live in Dr Disney's house in George Street & the plan of going to London is quite given up. No Rent or anything else can be extracted from them. Such misery never was known & yet surprising is it to see that these very people who are so soon to be levelled with the greatest poverty indulge in the most insufferable pride haughtiness & insolence –

The meek Mrs Crossley91 is reported as being very imperious & to have a strong touch of this malady which so unnecessarily prevails in the Greenup family they are much more on the decline than when you last saw them & from a gentleman who is likely to know having on account of their inability to pay given up all exchange of business with then speaks of it as impending & even at the doors – I meant yesterday to have gone there & as I got half way the rain was so violent as to drive me back again –

I don't like to neglect or slight people in their distress when they most need a Friend this is far from having real humanity & for all poor Mrs Greenup has trampled so upon the rules & maxims of decorum I shall pity & feel concerned about them. Short is this life & let us all try while we are in it to love & benefit each other – so many scenes & pictures of the vast mutability of this Earthly tabernacle have quite brought me to the seminal view of things- If the feeling can act as a stimulus to good actions I am happy.

I do feel sometimes I have curbed a vast deal that once grew out on all sides of my character deformed & unpleasing.

I should like to dispute with you if I durst against your maintaining that Laura was married I think in this work I've read, Mrs Dobson's Life &c was adverted to, & controverted, by several notes which appear highly plausible – She was 13. I know when Petrarch saw her for she was in the Church of St Claire at Avignon 1327 at 6 o'clock on the morng & it is singular enough that very day, hour, in that very Tower & in ye year 1348 as he describes it "this Light, this Sun withdrew from ye World- & on Good Friday also – But you must be much more highly informed on the subject than myself therefore I say no more – Zimmerman is in yr way of thinking & perhaps it may be an advantage I think that as he was a foreigner He might know with much more certainty than any here – The country being so much more contiguous to the place so memorable for the events of such a character – Mrs Johnson's work is I am sorry to say not in our Library.

The Thomsons will be stationary I believe – Miss Mary, as you assume, I wonder how she will fare not worse I should think than she has done the ruin of the Hodgsons will not affect her admittance or welcome in ye old Doctor's house.

I hear that poor Miss A. has been a little deranged but I trust it may not be of long continuance – your sympathing [sic] heart will dear L feel a spark of pity and regret I am sure it will; do you know I share with you in no little degree of it & if they come down to the Town I shall certainly call & be as polite if not more so than before –

I do think that never have the fears & distress of yr relatives arrived at such a pitch as now about Sam92 - the Lad will be resolute I am afraid a little refractory & if his Friends contest it with him I fear the result; you will think me rather rude to yr Brother but I really wish he were gone either for his own good or another or others - Disney's marriage looks like a retribution to them all –

I admire straw colour for your gown & shall say that you've desired me to tell yr Aunt that you have fixed upon the colour –

Don't on any account forget my dear the forthcoming message. Mrs Bramley – Mrs Veitch's Sister - requests as a particular favour of you to purchase for her at the Tunbridge Shop a Knitting needle case of plain wood, innumerable are to be met with I know at Doughty's, therefore by yr Father I hope this article may arrive before her departure.

Mrs Gervaise A. has asked me several times to Tea, & as often I have been engaged, she is rather what I call a pushing character & she does the rudest & most ignorant things sometimes possible –

Mrs Veitch was given a short letter for you which I enclose.

If the day be fine send Sam to see the Minster Castle and other curiosities of York. To Miss Swann pray don't be uncivil, she means well & has a mighty itching to be intimate with you both secretly & publicly she always styles you Lister & talks at a consequential rate as if you'd been long friends & cronies; all have their failings & vanity aspects of it is hers.

Mrs Swann has as you know steps to her door.

Have you ever seen ye Telford's? They are accomplished & pleasing, Tom Telford is well I hope - your good Father looks with longing delight, I daresay, to seeing you.

Yr Mother last night would not pay you ye compliment saying she felt our loss upon which we had a good humoured quarrel. Your absence is so severely felt by myself & I cannot but think by every individual of yr family – delightful still is the reflection that you are so happily situated –

I know you are worshipping Mr Duffin & can you have a better Idol – punctual no doubt to every wish of his & imbibing every intellectual advantage – The Country if you go into it will be highly useful - Dear little Willm. Crompton will be pastime for you sometimes –

My Servant is pretty, young & graceful, there are charms which cause me the closest attention – She is clever, quiet & exactly suited to me, with as far as I can judge an uncommon sweet temper, very clean. She is as I told you before but 17 - & not free from pulmonary delicacy –

Excuse my mutilated sheet dear L, I never am punctilious with you –

Marian I can certainly affirm is very often & much oftener than before a good deal improved & wears a handsome appearance – I have told her that I have informed you of this circumstance as an incentive to further amendment – Miss Swann's letter is open for yr perusal after which close & send it –

The measure of my stories before now lavished upon you to ye dregs & I must bid my Friend Farewell – Petitioning at ye same time another & another continuance of epistolatory kindness towards me, which can only be ye reward of my amiable submission to this sad separation, which is not fled from thy remembrance, but often reminds me that without a Friend & such a Friend too I should be in the vale of Tears a solitary sorry Being – Extracting sweets from gourds, which sometimes I vainly try, but after every abortive Trial exclaim none can supply the happiness of my life but my dear darling Lister

To whom I subscribe myself Ever most affectionately, E. Raine

(Written to me at Mr D's Micklegate York immediately on my arrival there in May 1811 aft. ye ver. severe illness from which I had just recovered —)

    Many families had lost everything after the recent collapse of the banks.93 Bankruptcy before the introduction of limited liability involved selling every single possession of the whole family94. Most families could not subsequently find anywhere to live and were sent to debtor's jail until their debts were paid. This normally meant the rest of their lives would be spent in abject poverty. Anyone who knew them previously would 'cut' them publicly since their 'station in life' had altered, just as Eliza was urged to 'cut' her sister because of changed circumstances.

At the end of May Eliza made her gratitude to Anne for helping her to move away from Lady Crawfurd clear. She bought presents to send by coach, including some plants to be paid for on arrival. Anne was to ask Mr Duffin, still in charge of Eliza's funds, to deduct seven shillings for these from his ward's quarterly allowance before sending it to her.

Wednesday May 30. 1810 12 o'clock noon95

My dear Lister

I hardly need tell you how happy I am made by your letter as you must be assured the perusal of it could not fail to make me completely so. I have now every pleasure processed for me that I could desire I am thankful indeed for it & I hope my future life will not be deficient in proving my gratitude & how highly I shall appreciate those blessings so very conducive to tranquil mind – first I should thank you all for your kind interest & Mr Duffin particularly for his indulgent compliance. You my dear have had much trouble about me but I thank you from my heart for it all & I hope you are assured of it.

I did not certainly expect such satisfactory information from you judge then how greatly increased was my pleasure on learning Miss Mellin's capability of accommodating me. So long is it since I have been accustomed to have all my wishes gratified that I began to expect no longer, but I have done wrong because it was forgetting to place confidence in the great giver of all good things. You have done all I could wish in reply to Miss G Mellins letter whatever Mr Duffin & you think right I comply with readily, & early regular hours will be beneficial to my recovery –

I am very well & fat & now shall be happy –

Lady Crawfurd has behaved better during the last week, I have nothing particularly to say of her than what you already know.

I have already executed your commissions but was too late for either the Lord Nelson or the Highflier96 however at 3 o'clock the Royal Charlotte passes through Doncaster, which I shall watch & deliver into the hands of the Guard with a strict

charge the Symphitum Asperinicus & a small parcel enclosing 5 pairs of silk stockings 2 pair of dress ones 3 pairs of walking ones with a bill of their amount. I have not attended quite to your desire that they should not exceed a certain price which you have named. I have ventured upon the dress ones a shilling higher & ye walking ones 2 higher also. If they are not large enough Mr Hopper will change them I have marked the whole number of them & hope they will suit you. Tell Miss Marsh who I know to be partial to this sort of attire (for well she may having such a beautiful ankle to sport) that the Duke of York lately ordered some beautifully fine Silk Stockings at a guinea & a half a pair which if she would like me to purchase for her I shall be happy to be commissioned.

As you & I never use ceremony dear L, I shall be obliged frankly to confess that yr order for the plants was as unexpected having ye other day thought some necessary things &

supposing I should have none other expences than yr letters till my next allowances, that I shall request you to send me if convenient a seven shilling piece in ye seal of Miss Pereira's letter as soon as you like& which little debt you must defray yourself less deducting it from my next quarterly allowance, when Mr Duffin sends it me which will you ask him to do a few days before the day for receiving it as I want to make a purchase of some silk stockings before I leave Doncaster. I make no apology for this act of freedom as you always tell me you like me better for them.

When you go into the country I shall not expect your letters so regularly as I have been accustomed to do knowing the uncertainty of conveyance to York. I shall generally write on a Friday as some of the Market people are usually going into town on Saturdays & will bring you my letter.

I approve of Miss Mellin's terms they are apparently reasonable. I hardly like the idea of your thinking of having me at Halifax till ye commencement of next half year as I am sure if it is so your Mother will inconvenience herself very greatly as I know as well as you that you have hardly room for yrselves much less for me in addition having had an increase to your domestic establishment lately. I almost think I might or had better remain here which I would do though I will not deceive you in saying I could bear it at all quietly being far too conscious of the misery of Lady C's temper which I feel to dread as some cruel enemy.

I received a letter from India a duplicate of one of Mr Parkin's former ones it brought to my memory my unfortunate Sister of whom I think as little as possible – Whenever Mr Duffin hears of her I hope you will communicate to me dear Lister for still I have a hankering to know how she is going on.

The weather is so oppressively hot that I am melted in my pelisse & shall cast it off in June hitherto I have walked in a morng after breakfast it being unsupportable at midday& even then I am overpowered but I dare not transgress Mr Duffin's order. I walk in the fields by myself for 2 hours & then a short while with Lady Crawfurd. How sorry I am to hear of Mrs Duffin's severe cold I had no idea of her having been confined so long I hope in yr next to hear of her entire recovery.

I pity the sad situation you so feelingly my dear friend describe of Mr Norcliffe's son[97] I cannot wonder that it recalls to your heart your dear deceased brother who I hope is in a happier state & rejoicing at his early release from a carnal World like this.

You can from sad experience commiserate in Miss Norcliffe's sufferings & offer her that consolation you are so capable of giving but do not allow the recollection to sadden your private hours when I know you feel all the bitterness of affectionate regret. – I am glad you like Miss Norcliffe she was a favourite rather with me from my short acquaintance with her but now I like her better since she has become so high in your estimation.

If you can tell me how Mr Whitaker & his better half are for I wish to inform Mrs Percival[98] but say not a word to them of my enquiries.

You may perceive by my scrawl I am hurried I fear missing the Coach which I hope will deliver to you at the same time this parcel as well as the Plants –

Lady C had four young people to dinner on Thursday last, she is in expectation of Mrs Haxby & her Mother some day next week & Mrs Willis & family also. The direction of the household concerns is as usual which you are aware is not the best in the World but I have nothing to do with it now & therefore never interfere.

I am amusing myself with an abridgment of the history of England & find from it both pleasure & profit. –

The 4 weeks I have to spend in a place become obnoxious to me I think will soon pass away when I know the comfort that awaits me at Halifax. I have become insensible Lister & I think stupid from my dull hours & unvaried manner of life & if it was not for the real delights of reading & occupying my mind I should be lost – I think of things till my mind is wearied & I am convinced a long continuance with Lady C would render me unfit for society – yesterday supposing you were preparing for Red House in my morning ramble I thought of you all & the pleasure you will find at Red House.

There is a sad object of compassion opposite here Miss Vernon's youngest daughter at whom often look & wonder how I can repine when I know her to be suffering the worst of misery & ill usage she is perfectly deformed from the conduct of her mother who beats her so unmercifully & is guilty of other inhuman acts that medical aid is often sent for to afford relief to the suffering girl. I wish often I could speak to her when I meet her & give her consolation but decorum will not permit it.

Now good bye my dear & very much loved friend. Give my best love & thanks to Mr & Mrs Duffin & Miss Marsh – Excuse my haste & Believe me with the most firm attachment

Yours sincerely   E. Raine   Remember me to all my friends & as I wish.

By Royal Charlotte May 30th 1810

   She left Lady Crawfurd's residence on June 3rd, having sent her globe and her piano in advance, and went first to Red House. Anne was there, and Miss Marsh joined them five days later. After a fortnight Anne returned to York and Eliza went there too to visit her good friend Mrs Swann, until the night of July 30th, when she took the coach to Halifax. After a good sleep on arrival at the Mellins' in Halifax, she had tea with Mrs Weatherherd and dinner with the Misses Mellin. She was overjoyed to be moving closer to the Lister family and anticipated living there with Anne very soon.

   But Anne had already tacitly decided never to return to Halifax and she regretted her pledge of undying love. She was becoming very friendly with Isabella Norcliffe, the eldest daughter of a very prosperous family who lived in Langton Hall, a manor set in its own village and estate in the beautiful rolling wolds of the East Riding on the road to Malton. Mrs Norcliffe was a local judge by descent. The family had extensive connexions within local society, from tenants on their land to the military and judiciary. During term

Isabella, or Tib as she was known, lived at her father's town house at Petergate in the city, just a short walk from the Manor School. Isabella was not only rich; she thought of herself as masculine, just like Anne. They experimented accordingly, their eyes on the future. Not only was Anne physically inclined towards Tib, she was also madly in love with another classmate, Mariana Belcombe. She reported to Tib:

"I like her for your sake, and I wish I knew her more to like her better."[99]

Mariana, the daughter of a wealthy doctor, lived in Petergate opposite Isabella. Both liked Anne for sparkling wit, courage, passion and sexuality, and as second in line to inherit she was far more acceptable than previously. Nevertheless she did her best to involve Eliza with her new friends since she was potentially of the same rich class.

"I love you with the truest & most sincere affection, doat upon every word you utter & think myself one of the most fortunate human beings in possessing such a Friend.

Thank you my dearest Girl for yr kind enquiries after Mariana I hear from her Sisters she is quite well though from herself I have not heard for a length of time; there is I fear no chance of her returning till February.

I gave your message to Mr & Mrs Duffin who desire their love in return.

And now my beloved Girl it is high time to conclude which I shall do by saying that I shall never cease to remain your grateful & affectionate

Friend Isabella Norcliffe

You do not mention your Friend Miss Raine I hope she is well. Do not forget to give my love to her. "

Anne had recently joined the newly established York Friendly Society, and had begun to take more care of her appearance, even worrying about her shoes.[100] In her new life she would have to look respectable. Would Eliza's dark appearance be detrimental? There was also the issue of Jane, now an impecunious 'native' 'fallen' woman in the process of having a bastard child. Neither had any important friends or relatives. The exotic nature of their Indian background had faded completely, and so had the lure of their riches. There were no letters between Anne and Eliza till the following year.

That summer Anne arranged a meeting between Isabella and Eliza. If the two got on with each other, if Eliza could be included, perhaps Anne could keep her as a friend. Isabella was in no doubt about the role that Eliza would play. Eliza wrote about Isabella in secret code:

"How can I refuse my darling husband's solicitude to hear the events of Isabella's visit? Nothing glaringly strange took place, my love, but …it may illustrate most clearly the near resemblance that dear creature has arrived at to you. In entering I was accosted

rather roughly; we sat down, and after looks that really now, L, made me blush, the tray was brought in. She ate heartily and drank freely, insisting on my drinking your health with all the airs of masculine fervour, forgot everything she had to say and spoke more in her eyes than I liked; put her hand into her habit; sat with all the freedom of a man, and thought, I daresay, that she could not be too near to me.

These are singular traits, L …and the consciousness of a certain something, being but human nature, occurred to me so strongly as to influence me to the elevation of my dignity…. Or the consequences would have inclined me to rudeness….

After this she would make me read your letter. I hesitated, feeling the warmth of your expressions, only fit for the eye of matrimonial love…. After the perusal she smiled and a repetition was increased of many acts so resembling thine, as to make me ask my husband whether he had been so unfortunately candid as to have disclosed our marriage, love and attachment?101

I asked after Mariana Belcombe, at which she gave me the strangest look and said, "What makes you ask me after her?" and I replied "Merely from the idea of her great intimacy… "In future I shall learn discretion in communicating to my friend, finding that she tells you everything."

Anne wrote back in strong terms to deny that she had any relationship with Mariana. She had told her York friends nothing about the closeness of her relationship with Eliza or their mutual promises, and failed to mention to her future 'wife' that she was having a physical relationship with Isabella. Guiltily she demanded an apology, which Eliza abjectly supplied.102 Mollified, Anne returned to Halifax to stay overnight with Eliza at the Mellins' lodgings and make up their differences, causing her mother to be angry at the impropriety and to demand that Anne should stop seeing her there.

Anne's friendships with Isabella and Mariana continued unabated, visits to one and another interspersed with letters referring to health and exercises, all veiled references to sex. They did not use secret code. Although Anne invented a new code of consonants and punctuation marks for Isabella, she only tried to use it once.

Meanwhile Eliza set about her new life in Halifax. For two weeks in September she stayed with former school friends in St Helens, Lancashire. On her return she attended Mrs Rebecca Lister's birthday party and renewed her affection for Anne's brother Sam, who took her home whenever she went out. She resumed her "*literary employment*" and French and made numerous visits to Northgate and Shibden Hall. She was really happy to be with the Lister family again.

Anne was sent home in October with scarlet fever, and Eliza nursed her for months. On the 19th Miss Maria Alexander returned from Sunderland with her friend Miss Hodson, and in November Eliza dined with them and Miss Mary Thomson at the Alexanders' house, even though she had a sore throat and cough and was mourning the death of young princess Amelia on the 22nd November. Having so much to do Eliza gave up keeping her diary; the last entry was on November 11th. She was so happy that Anne was at home.

Scarlet fever kept Anne in Halifax all winter. She returned to school the following April and stayed for eighteen months. Eliza had become her best informant about Halifax life.

Anne's sister Marian, wrote Eliza, had been deeply worried that her elder sister would die of the fever; Anne's mother and other ladies were resuming their earlier attempts at match-making on Eliza's behalf, and the wealthy Priestleys were the current favourites. Edward Priestly of Cliff Hill, who would eventually "*have all Mrs Walker's fortune*", had been making eyes at her. Some favoured the elder Priestley at White Windows, though Mrs Greenup preferred "*young Edwards*" of Pye Nest. Eliza was very flattered to receive such attention but refused to succumb. Mrs Lister complained that she was "*too choosy*"; she was nearly past marriageable age at 19 and it was time that her life was sorted out. Maria Duffin had by now become a governess since she had no dowry; Jane Boulton had vanished from polite society; Anne Lister intended to be a writer; Sam Lister was to join the Army as an Ensign in a few months. What did Eliza intend to do with her life? But Eliza kept her secret to herself: she considered herself more than ever Anne's wife.

Anne's exercise book containing entries from 22nd February 1810 to 13th August 1816 is lost. But without doubt that summer of 1810 was one of the best in their lives.

1811

Mrs Rebecca Lister had other urgent considerations. The continuing economic slump caused by the Napoleonic War had exacerbated Captain Lister's inability to raise rents from his tenants. Consequently they had decided to sell all their estates in Yorkshire to live in Devonshire; only rich, elderly Lister retainers would stay in Halifax at Northgate and Shibden Hall. Mrs Lister was known to drink too much, and Jeremy was well known both for his lack of social graces and for drinking with the lower classes at disreputable dens; they could start a new life at a lower social level.

Rebecca was also distressed about Sam. She hated the idea of her mild, quiet, gentle, timid son joining the army and put all possible obstacles in his way. In any case the family couldn't afford to buy him a commission.

The slump had affected other families too, like the Bramleys who were bankrupt and the Crossleys and Greenups who were far less affluent.103 In the midst of all their misery Eliza was to be seen leading a happy, bustling, financially secure life, buying a straw-coloured gown for Anne and joking about her new servant's "*pulmonary delicacy*". She quite forgot to tell Anne about the knitting-case she had promised to buy for Mrs Bramley104 even though the Bramleys had been told to quit their house by June and were too ashamed to speak to neighbours in the street. In any case Anne was living a life of luxury in York and could soon expect a fortune as a dowry.

Resentment was bound to erupt. Mrs Greenup made acid comments about Anne, so Eliza felt it her duty to defend her. (Afterwards she repeated Mrs Greenup's advice to Anne, to play less chess because it made her seem so masculine and she was sure it would injure a woman's brain.)

The Listers meanwhile broke out in quarrels about money, Sam and their future, although within a month some rents were actually paid, so the Listers were suddenly able to remain in Halifax. Other problems waned too. Sam's enlistment was put off for a year at his mother's request. The Bramleys moved in with relatives. Eliza, anxious to be part of the family, took over the schooling of Sam and Marian Lister, giving them "*drill*" daily. Dr Disney Alexander, the consummate bachelor, suddenly announced that he was to marry.

Eliza did not waver from her devotion to Anne in financially difficult times, when pocket money was not forthcoming, and kept on sending her money; £5 in June, £30 in July.105 She wrote the amounts in code to make sure that Mr Duffin did not see.106

When the school's term ended in July Anne finally did return to Halifax. The usual correspondence between Anne and Eliza stopped when they were together.

Halifax May 15. 1811. Wednesday night after 9

I should scarcely have written to you dear L. before receiving an answer to my last packet had not the case of Mrs Bramley required it; for her you may remember I commissioned you to purchase something of a knitting or netting case, which I had repeated by yr Father with a letter etc., but he is returned unaccompanied by anything of ye kind and I begin to despair of your observance to my wish without a gentle hint of this kind; on my own account I could have rested satisfied but ye business of others is of consequence & should be expeditiously executed.

I therefore proceed to beg you will my dear if not by return of post sometime this week or not later than next Monday send me ye required article ye directions for which look in my last in a parcel, with a letter to Mrs Veitch written in yr true style of elegance & sublimity as a little pride on ye account of my Friend makes one particularly desirous that Mrs

Bramley an excellent judge & critic should see ye fair & brilliant productions of yr epistolatory powers. She is really an agreable woman, rarified in genius & uncommon in cultivation acquainted with examining Authors most intimately & possesses a general delightful fund of entertainment –

She I hope will one day be known to you & you will admire her with me I am sure such a woman; & will not my dear L. be further pleased to hear that upon me she had really bestowed no light Encomiums, I am declared a very good favorite & the following will illustrate the pleasure that she can find in E.R., "There is no young woman whom conversation has pleased me so much as Miss R's."

Such a remark from a common character would not affect me, but from an enlightened mind it flatters me & stimulates to that mental enlargement which daily I find so necessary & proves ye source of my present & best happiness – Without my Books I am lost, ye once ignorant & careless Eliza Raine – Now I long for every hour of that conversation with you which In feel I have estimated too slightly - If I did not know that it would be drawing you away from yr greatest happiness & advantage I should say Lister do return to me never should I enjoy yr society so much as now –

Thank Miss Marsh my dearest L. for her kind intention of writing in answer to my last which has been communicated to me by Mrs Greenup ys morning a delightful pleasure Lister because you ye subject of her goodness are expatiated upon, a pleasure which vainly I look from you – Heaven Lister gives me Friends from whom we draw much much consolation; never have you found me unwilling to afford you every request of such a fortune, but resignation is my only resource & I never again shall demand of you so irksome a task -

Mrs Greenup is certainly conscious that she has done wrong; when I entered she was confused & distant; I saw no list, no railing as upon all other occasions they were slumbering, & you were a point fearingly avoided by us in conversation; once she happened to say Miss Lister is delightful full of character & excellent, I said yes Mrs Greenup without speciousness, possessing wisdom & not abusing it, [-]ing to injure either by word or deed the humblest of her creatures, & possessing a Christian heart that leads rather to ye forgiveness of her enemies than resentment - I thought I would strike a little, my dear she coloured up furiously & then in defiance for she seemed to think defence necessary & imagining I levelled premeditatedly at her, she said there are characters in whom we are deceived & who make a cloak of candour for many internal vices, much deception & much ambition –

After this and a little more we talked prettily many a fine speech was made to me many a request that I would be a frequent visitor at Darcy Hey to which I returned distant thanks & never accepted of one of them –

She knows it that I can't endure her. I never remembered you to her or mentioned any friendliness from you towards Miss Norcliffe's passing thro Halifax as she did without calling on her a disagreeable occurrence to Mrs G I know, & the slight insinuations I *gave such as I heard a vast deal of Mrs G's visit to York indeed Miss M was quite entertaining in her various communications & have a little opened to her that I am influenced by them, she does not want discrimination & I am willing in this instance to aid it –*

However no more of this disagreeable character further than she wants to hear if Captn Lally has fortune if they have left York & indeed all the news about them you can send –

Mrs G talks of going to Doncaster races, & I fancy of taking her daughter or daughters with her –

Ever since you went dear L. I have been constantly visiting & for the last fortnight daily & hourly have I been employed in this way, this Evening I drank tea at Mrs Veitch's, yesterday I walked to S. Hall to ask yr Worthy Aunt & Uncle to dinner for Friday this long promised visit & in ye evening I have all the families. The meeting will be agreeable as I love all yr family.

Yr Mother is really dejected about Sam, they often quarrel about this taste for ye army, they think oppositely as you may imagine, the Lad is more & more eager & his Mother as much so miserable – He improves & I get quite attached to him he is so like you & his temper is benevolent & amiable – Tiresome lad he has nothing to say of you, indeed he scarcely had an opportunity of seeing you so I hear the game at chess was preferable to a few protracted moments of yr Father's society –

I beg you will not play frequently you have often to my observation suffered much from the anxiety naturally caused by it, & who would allow a pleasure at the expence of health –

At Crow Nest I met Miss Park Mrs John Hunter's bridesmaid a very agreable elegant woman we conversed much & I parted from her company with regret I met her at ye New Church on Sunday when we greeted each other most cordially indeed L; all my Friends are particularly kind & treat me with uncommon freedom & friendship –

Mrs Briggs I also met & found her exactly what you had represented – The Bramleys find in them excellent friends - & indeed they seem to be surrounded by many of similar worth – Mr Hudson has offered to educate ye boys not to board them – Report says that ye Crow Nest Walkers have requested them to take up their residence awhile there or one of their cottages for present shelter.

A Miss Hawkins who was staying at ye Shay last summer & who lives in Wales offers an Asylum to all ye family – Whether all this be true is not for me to declare – Miss Bramley & all of them hear the calamity with great submission & are unchanged in all respects & points of their character – I saw her ye other day on Cagill's walk where I sauntered & when she stared at me with confident assurance I passed & pitied!

Mrs Hodgson is recovering fast & I fancy their state is not so deplorable as I pictured to you – They coming into ye Country & a rumour that Mr Hodgson is joining in a Foundery

Concern near Leeds –107The Bramleys must quit their House by ye 10th of June –Miss Hudsons my dear waited on me yesterday to my astonishment –

By this time my well beloved you will have received a letter from Miss Hannah Hudson who as yr Uncle of S. Hall humourously remarks is proving to you that she also will direct her first epistolatory effort to one that gratitude alone would demand. My predictions all fulfill –

Dear dear Lister you are unconscious that many are persuaded there exists between you the most intimate Friendship when I know how things are – I smiled & simpered when I heard your direction asked from yr Mother, she really looked so surprised I am afraid ye Hudsons would see it – Be polite & answer by return of post pray –

Did I ever mention an invite from Mrs Paley to Tea & Mr Veitch says I should have received one for dinner had not Mrs P wished to pay that Compliment to older Friends –

Dr Thomson is going to purchase a House it is said near Gervaise Alexander's on the same side of Hope Hall & some one else said that one near H bridge108 lately occupied by ye dissenting Minister109 was likely to be made choice of –

My dear since yr Father was at Weighton I have been consoling yr Mother by day & by night I've seldom slept at home. For our amusement I got Zelues110 & read it aloud & it has highly pleased us & in a great miasma diverted the melancholy of yr dear Mother on Sam's account – I am very merry & am an everlasting talker you will think me altered when you next see me –

Sophocles' tragedies I have endeavoured to read but dissipation alas obstructs every purpose – a young Stansfield with Mr Wigglesworth has fallen admiring me & protected by Mrs Veitch hopes for ye honor of visiting me both morning & at my early parties he is a nice young man I believe & very sensible –

Tother day as I was walking I saw a gentleman at sight of me stop on ye opposite side & gaze what I call properly romantically, his eyes gushing with love & admiration – I happened to be entering a poor woman's cottage & this posture lasted till I came out when he attended me at a proper distance to my lodging with attitudes various & suitable to express his passion. This same youth is very young Mr Stansfield – Ought I not to be vain he was to have met me ys Evening but he was called out of Town –

I have occupation enough for my thoughts L, I am hurried with noise, racket & engagements, yet this suits me I think & has forced from me that exertion which I never should have called forth voluntarily –

you are my dearest Lister, one ever dear to my remembrance, I love you & enjoy you now only in retrospection, I believe I have attained to a Virtue, I have attained that which prefers your happiness to my own for tho' I must necessarily feel that a sad vacuum remains yet allow myself not to imagine I can be at all unhappy whilst you are so superlatively so. I should like to hear when you think it likely for our seeing you.

Sam goes in a month or two – I wish you would ask Mr Duffin whether he will not think of this Winter passed in Halifax a dangerous experiment for yr delicate Health my dr Lister, you are certainly tender as its possible & even in case of your amendment during ye Summer will not ye bleak airs of this Country throw you back – This anxious point to my heart perhaps Miss Marsh will communicate when she means me the great pleasure of hearing from her –

Thanks to yr Isabella adored for her love & when you scribble next to her return it most kindly – I do like her & I am rejoiced at her safe arrival - May she live long years of happiness & solace by all the generous ties of yr firm friendship & I believe that this is now necessary to her happiness. Unceasing lecture to her upon her health & I shall follow ye bright example to my dear prudent Friend –

Think of its value Lister & think of those individuals who would lay down their lives for the [-] of yours I am amongst that devoted number & certainly if I lost you the rest of my days would appear a blank forever! Singular possession & form Gods knows as ever Friendship was in its Golden days. You are one of those unfortunate characters regardless of yourself when divided from Mr Duffin who is ye only one on Earth as weak say so to whom you will pay unbounded obedience cannot this amiable property be transferred a little –

{Do dear husband tell me if ps111 has ever taken place since you went to York my eagerness to know is torture oh dear??? do satisfy me}112 to those equally desirous I am sure to promote yr good but perhaps only equal to ye imitation of his precepts from where we derive oh what unfading consolation I sigh when I reflect on it as if one burdened with the weight of obligation –

He is a good man is a Father to you –

I will not forget a nasty speech of Mrs Greenup's I spoke of yr being universally noticed and that ye whole Town has called on you & she said "The people indeed are always in 2 extremes they as easily & do as frequently lay aside their favourites as they caress them – It is what I term said she a rage for a new comer which soon dies." Upon which I said you speak from experience I daresay & therefore I don't dispute it – My dear I am of course annihilated in her good opinion forever! –

Good night my taper is dying – God bless you & whilst in this life may you [have] uninterrupted health & happiness this is the incessant wish spring from ye heart of me for ye present E. R. –

Thursday morning 10 o'clock No letter from you –

What glorious weather & do you not enjoy it! The shades of Red House are not at all more propitious to my hiding from you than the smoke of ye grown – I suppose the Body & Beard & Zephyrs a meandering stream have of all engaging Charms – however I beg that amidst all these delights of nature you will write to me I am anxious that before the consummation of a fortnight I should not have to exclaim what a tedious period of silence as your partner

I have thrown off my Wintry garb & sport about in the thinnest attire, I suffer not in any way but am fat & well liking – Ralph Leybride's[113] adventures is reckoned a good burlesque upon novels –

I must some day soon drag myself up to Hipperholme but shall take my time Mr John Greenup the military gentleman has been here for six weekends & left them yesterday –

Pray send me word where you have put my Nankeen Black velvet Boots I can't find them – Yr thirst for news you say is insatiable only after ye perusal of this scrawl it will be amply quenched – I have taken leave of my natural style because I know others hear all – that I say if you blame me Dispute the cause to yourself – However to you all I beg my kindest love … Believe me dearest Lister Humbly Yours E. R.

Young Saltmarshe is here – The Lees are coming to Southampton –

We are all mighty [--] concerning you & Captn Taylor – I desire your picture may be sent me this you must not return without – you've never talked to yr Father about returning home –

Miss Philip's lover has neglected her … {tell me what money you have}[114] Miss Bramley is coming … Adieu –

I have just had Mrs Bramley, Veitch & young Stansfield he really is a sensible man – Yr letter is arrived to yr Mother … Miss Prestons of Green Royd called just now –

My dear Lister Anything you want we will send you [--] we bountiful?

Wednesday June 5th 1811 near 6 o'clock[115]

How long is it since I wrote to you, well may you exclaim & sincerely do I do ye same with remorse of conscience; you never doubt my affection therefore you will not have been so unkind as to impute my silence to such a cause. Lister you know me too well to imagine that my attachment for you can know any diminution & either from absence or any other of these fluctuating occurrences of this life. In the heat of noise of bustle or in the bosom of retirement or solitude the image of my dear dear Friend remains perfect to my remembrance, perfect to my heart & unchanged.

A reason shall you have for my hitherto silence; it has arisen solely from the uninterrupted gaiety I have been obliged to enter into; this is a compliance that we must bestow on Custom & the regulation of Fashion –

Ever since ye receipt of your first long letter I have been immersed in one continued dissipation. Sometimes the scene has been pleasantly varied by my passing a few days at your House, & frequently dining there singly; the Sunday previous to ye 21st of last Month & ye day on which yr long letter arrived I slept at North Bridge as well as on

Monday; Tuesday I remained to celebrate yr dear Brother's birthday & returned in ye Evening after drinking Tea at Mrs Weatherherd's –

Since I have passed my time alternately at different Houses one day I was asked to Darcy Hey with ye offer of a Bed this I declined & preferred going to yr House – on ye 20th we all met at Northgate to celebrate ye anniversary of yr Aunt's natal day, when Mrs Veitch & Weatherherd, Mr Wigglesworth were asked in addition – On Monday last I dined at S. Hall & yr dear Aunt accompanied me to Hipperholme. Miss Hannah116 was to be seen & informed us she had written to you on ye Saturday previous. I could scarcely preserve a tranquil visage & perhaps your punctitious Aunt could with great difficulty do ye same Miss Martha & I were ye loquacious & I find her most agreable … You scarcely know how they have represented yr kindness –

I caused a little astonishment at Dr Paley's where Mrs William Priestley117 was & who is well acquainted with ye Hudsons, when speaking of ye different Characters of ye 3 daughters I said "some imagined Miss Hudson ye cleverest & I fancied I had heard Miss Lister say that Miss Martha had ye pre-eminence in this respect, but indeed (added I) Miss Lister does not pretend to be an adequate judge as she is not sufficiently acquainted with ye family to form an opinion" –

I am one of those my dear who wish to undeceive erroneous conjecture & when I hear opinions drummed into my ear, when I know their falsity I generally attempt to clear away ye error – you will excuse me for thus assuming to myself upon a topic that should perhaps be alone Yours, but when my Friend is not present to defend herself I take upon myself, & I think only consistent with ye attribute of Friendship to be deputy – But farewell to ye subject, only first let me beg you will let me have ye copy of yr letter to Hannah H, & some day shew me her epistle.

This morning brought me an epistle from Mrs Frances Swann, with every satisfactory account of yourself, the Truth of it I am inclined to credit as I hope you would not be allowed to lie to your York Friends on the subject of health or rather you durst not for fear of such ready detection –

Happy am I that you are progressively amending long may you continue to blessed Friend of my heart for whom every telling ye most exquisite is ever alive, of course all was immediately communicated to yr Friends who appeared to participate in ye joy –do do take care of yourself –

How can you be inclined to scold me for writing to Miss Marsh I feel every ache or pain of yours cause of sufficient alarm & if by chance you should have a little occasional debility or a little of any thing else I am sure you will pardon an inquietude that urges me to write & express my suspicions it is a fact Lister that you have so long deceived me in regard to yr health that I have quite given up all credibility – The hour of reformation is long by & I never more shall look for it –

I was you will imagine a visitor at Mrs Paley's yesterday Evening – where were ye Walkers of Crow Nest Cliff Hill, ye Waterhouses, Mrs W. Priestley, Prestons etc. etc. – I was most politely received & ye Walker's kindness to me is exceeding –

I could not judge much of Mrs W. Priestley as she was very silent –

Dr Paley I find out makes ye 2d gentleman in this neighbourhood & never another could I find excepting young Saltmarshe who is not personally known to me, but who sits opposite to me at Church every Sunday & certainly wears ye externals of one –

Mrs Paley on my taking leave in company with good Mrs Veitch, requested me particularly to be a frequent visitor & these invitations were accompanied with such a probability of Truth, that I purpose going sometimes in a familiar way.

Mrs Veitch has just now been here & sends her kindest love & if perfectly convenient to my dear Lister would thank you to send the parcel with my little et ceteras by ye end of this week or not later than Tuesday in ye next, as she wishes to have then before her visit to Wakefield which takes place the latter end of the week after -

Now then my beloved L, you will be fussed, a letter & a long one I will have, another there must be for Home, for S. Hall & a short scribble surely for Mrs Veitch, & pray write to Samuel he wishes me to put you in mind of a Locket you promised him with your valuable Hair enclosed. Mrs Veitch mentioned that she intends herself ye pleasure of answering yr last in ye course of time –

Now let me announce a pleasing piece of news! Samuel, the ever amicable Samuel, at ye strong solicitation of yr Mother, when it was represented to him, the distress of his relatives his own delicacy of health & little likelihood of surmounting the hardships of the Camp, has like a truly philanthropic son given up the idea of it118 till next Spring – Marian's delight was so unruly that it had like to have cost you ye postage of a letter so eager was she to give you immediate communication. His friends are pleased both at his amiable forbearance & the probable rather certain pleasure of his remaing amongst them – Your Mother wrote to you my dear L & explained my taciturnity I hope – the letter I daresay was acceptable –

Ere I moved to anything of myself let me give you ye news of ye country – The Bramleys are removed. Mr & Mrs B occupy old Doctor's house till the family return which will be in a few weeks. Miss Bramley is gone to Crow Nest for a few weeks – In ye Autumn she & her Sister Marian are to visit her Friend Miss Hawkins benifitted by country air –

For ye benifit of Sam I let him have my library books, Marian steals a few also sometimes – I drill them occasionally Samuel improves vastly under my tuition. Marian is rather unruly, Sam is mentally stifled of late particularly – I must tell you Marian degenerated, & is not going on so well as formerly she wants your precepts & yr example, she is headstrong & vulgar, but don't say a word of it to any. Your brother will ever do honor & credit to yr ancient Family as well as yourself, Marian wants much tutoring – your Mother reports me as giddy to you my dear, I am so in her society & have been particularly of late, she was very low about Sam & was getting melancholy, but since this change in affairs the dismality is changed into merrimality & I have bid adieu to my volatility –

a fortnight ago young Thompson of Leeds called & drank Tea with me unasked, his visits are rather too frequent, a young woman in my unprotected situation is imprudent in admitting such conduct therefore I have ordered him never more to be admitted –

Yr Mother sadly wants me to be married called me a prude, but finding many approvg my determination & on reflection agreeing to its reasonableness herself she has changed her tone & become my votary; What are ye intentions of Mr Thompson by thus acting, whether honorable or not or of what species of Conduct I don't pretend to define, however I think he would not come so frequently without giving some light to his intentions if they were possessing any solid worth – I neither desire pleasure or improvement from him therefore he is by me finally discarded –

The Hodgsons are coming soon. Mr H is to heap up the business of the [-119] and that of Attorney jointly120 –

Don't laugh dear L but it is currently reported Miss Mary Thomson is going to marry old Doctor & that ye family are highly incensed as well they may if it is so, behold the hypocrite recovered, whom I long suspected & who has fully been fastened in the bosom of her Friend to sting her to death; have I, or hast thou most penetration sometimes L? I pretend not to yr logic, to your scholarship or science but thank God I can as readily detect vice & [-121] an impending evil –

Dr Disney is going to be married in a few days, he is to be translated to Heaven. He confesses that it is a marriage of prudence122 not love – poor man how he has been driven to rave about ye search of a mate to comfort his declining years & has lighted upon one truly at last, not we will say with the adornments of youth, beauty or loveliness but internal worth. I laughed at Hipperholme & said I thought the fervours of youth have long gone by with both of them. I sometimes laugh at the nonsense of garrulous age, they say ye old are oftner sillier than youth when engaged on the belligerent of love –

The Thomsons go to the House I described in yr vicinity –

Of ye trip to Devonshire, it depends I believe solely & entirely upon Mr Duffin if he pronounces it necessary, & unfit for yr trial of another winter here, your kind Father will I daresay pass the Winter in that delightful country, the air of which I suppose is as delightful or in a more moderate degree resembles that of Italy –

Oh! War123 that should thus prove hostile to our wishes & our hopes! Had it not waged so universally with such fury you would have been transplanted most likely to a more genial climate where how sincerely I wish you at present! A German resides in ye Town who often meets me a genteel appearance & noble air, what kindred sympathy I feel for all those alienated from their Mother Country! By ye by I hope young Mr Norcliffe or

George Crompton are alive, this last dreadful engagement sounds terrible in my ears & threatens Death to every Friend, alas what a melancholy thing if they fall victims!

How is dear Miss Norcliffe? She is yr Friend & of course dear to me too I hope, be kind very kind Oh my dear Mrs Duffin Lister she is excellent in heart & what do you not aver, how pleasing too to see youth respectful to age – Were she here I would be most happy, give to her & Mr Duffin … etc. my kindest remembrances – … adieu till after tea –

I surely have now run this my catalogue of newsy events & I will turn to Home to dear domestic enjoyment & myself! Sometimes I have had a little past time to read & have partly gone thro The History of England & last ended with ye reign of Henry 8th who in spite of his vices in his reign surely this country improved imperceptibly-

Sophocles is still by me & is not finished, I have neither got to Ajax Electra or Philactetes, for you must know that there is a long explanation of the Ancient Grecian Theatre, the rise progress & decay of tragedy & it is so interesting that I am detained a good deal by making notes – I suppose the last Tragedian Sophocles has united in his stile all the attributes of our Shakespeare indeed he seems stiled the Shakespeare of Antiquity –

Perhaps now that I am at rest I can diligently pursue French, resume drawing & reading frequently - There are many studies in which your peculiar aid is requisite to make me imbibe with facility - What say you to This "Self Controul" Mrs Frances Swann speaks of. She desires me to remind you of your omission of this her just & lately assumed title & commit no more such like errors –

You may rather expect a parcel from me in a short time, with some commissions etc. – I wish to my dear Miss Duffin124 ye other day as kindly as I could, may I ever be to her an invariable good Friend, I esteem her most highly –

I never was better in my life& am so strong & fat that I made yr Aunt Anne exclaim ye other day & she purposes writing ye history of my astonishing health to Mrs F. Swann & Miss M. of her kind promise to epistolarise to me soon the letter will be most welcome when it comes {125Don't say anything but Miss Swann says Miss Marsh is practising upon you her deceptions & that she has been assailed but has resisted & expresses some surprise at my feeling so obliged for her attentions to you which are alone ordered by selfish motives. For God's sake be cautious & equally prudent as ever & in every action, offerance let prudence guide you. Of course you are sometimes supposed to connive at their conduct & I have battles to fight to eradicate such notions. My darling husband will you stay the winter? When did ps126 take place, dear object of my love & best darling of all my thoughts? Why use such closeness with your wife, indeed I don't deserve it. Farewell my dear, dear lamented L, be well for my happiness. I meant to send you twenty pound in July but you shall hear again about it. I got your mother to send five pounds.}

Summer seems to have put on her best merits this Evening & I am going to enjoy ye sweets of a country walk by myself towards Stony Royd, I prefer now you are away there solitary pleasures.

Sam, Marian, & yr Father & Mother & I took a country walk ye other Evening & much I enjoyed –

The Bramley's sale has commenced & Mrs Greenup has purchased several articles

My poor Servant Grace by name & Grace by nature literally left me on Monday last, alas poor girl, in a deep consumption, & if a month's care at home & country air don't recover her I must dismiss her my service – I am fond of ye Girl in every respect & a few things at present … could have affected me so much , she had completely won my heart by her innocence, her humility, modesty & superior achievements for such a girl as considered of mean parentage . There are plenty anxious to come to me but I think her so valuable that if there's a chance for her I will have her back again –

Sam had little to say of his York jaunt at you he was very laconic – Hull he expressed a pleasure in seeing. He grows yr very image daily & of course a just excuse for having twined round my heart which he certainly has dear engaging lad. I am very wishful that … you may return to some delightful felicities in the Bosom of a Brother's Friendship - He is my really chief pleasure when I visit N. Bridge –

The L. are fond of me I believe, Marian is all caressing & Sam all attention to my wants. If I am ill that is to say sick, one prescribes kisses as a remedy & the other pleasing attentions. I am a little Goddess reigning there; great Juno herself could not be more powerful or more caressed by her subjects –

Good blessing dear till tomorrow – The morrow of your returning society when is that to me that day is perhaps far off – but I will never lament or enumerate my wants – As long as thou art happy Child I glory in mortification! You cannot be kinder to me than unremitting care of yourself.

Sometimes spend a thought about ye picture & let me have it instead of Sam, I am sure he will give it up to me – for if I do but distantly hint a wish he is all commission. I can get him to do anything –

At Night near 10 I have been pacing before the House by ye Ancient Trees listening to the … Clock chimes & after looking over yr letter find there are some things to answer – so I begin – I owe you for my watch, Yr adventure at Mrs W Oldfield's concerning Johnson surprises me - I approve the improvement & yr recovering of yr own watch –

I suppose Mary Swann is accomplished by Miss Walker's guiding her. Poor Mr Robert Swann & his accident! Do do be particular in mentioning whether yr debility is gone, do drink milk my darling you were always fond of it – Have yr secretions ever been? Have natural functions ever been suspended? …

I one day told Mrs Greenup of ye £3000 & ye acquiescence of old Townend to make his childhood equal – Mrs G is decked out superbly & impertinently asked yr Mother & Father when you were coming back –

Mrs Veitch wished to have the something for a Chimney piece of Spar, now you can't be puzzled.

Alas poor Selby! My first & earliest Friend, dear girls gone to be happier I hope. You know her too my dear but not so intimately as I did. What a short lived happiness. The living are to be pitied & lamented not the dead! –

Farewell my dearly loved L & may you & I each take a lesson from these awful dispensations of Providence – Let us live aright & we shall not fear to die.   Bless you my dear L & believe me yours truly E.R.

Thursday morng. I have just had an invitation from ye Prestons for next Monday Eveng. I propose havg. A party ye day after adieu my dear L

Thus ends a long, happy, well-articulated letter from Eliza in Halifax to Anne in York. Both were socially accepted in their respective spheres and both had a full list of contacts and events. Eliza was particularly looking forward to seeing Anne on her return at the end of the school term.

Halifax July 5th 1811127

On the borders of Greece I write; & therefore invoke the celestial deities to aid my pen; on Calafoie ground how can I fail!

The enigma is this: Mitford's History is supporting this paper & has given rise to my lofty strain –

Now my dear L I begin my letter to say how delighted I am with yours although written in the strain of melancholy which no wonder you feel at approaching separation from Friends you so dearly & so justly love; yet this very sadness is the foretaste of approaching joy to me & to numbers who really love & reverence you as much & … whose long tried Friendship to all around him calls forth the warmest & sincerest gratitude in hearts who love as you & I must do & ought to do ---

I feel for my darling Lister the conflict that is hastening on but as I know your superior mind is ever equal to its own consolation fortitude & support I have nothing to add but that I wish almost for your precious sake that it was over. To him to her to all of your Friends remember me most affectionately, indeed Lister I loved them so well as now – But I'll dismiss the subject & direct you by a few anecdotes of my present temporality ---

My good Grace is now with me returned to that best health I have so earnestly wished she is a jewel to me & who knows by her worth & uprightness she may for years remain my domestic ---

My dear sorrowing Mrs Veitch is rather more reconciled I drank Tea there on Wednesday your Aunt Anne & I are the only visitors admitted I believe ---

The Alexanders are arrived I sent to enquire after them for which mark of politeness they seemed obliged but Mrs A's health being bad no visitors are allowed – They go to the Sea soon

Disney's nuptials will soon be accomplished –

Your poor dear Mother is very ill but nothing more than one of her usual attacks in her stomach -

If you will really promise to be secret I'll tell you a secret – Your Mother has no pity from me being in a way that I imagine few married ladies but what look for ere

they enter that state – I am a great favorite & notwithstanding the bickering about the keys between us at the Conclusion after much argumentation I made her laugh & vexed to be thus triumphed over she said in a pet "you are such a queer girl I don't like you at all" The keys my dear therefore need be no source of wickedness to thee, they cannot be better of than in the hands of your good Father who truly philosophical looked on during the afore mentioned altercation with a calm smile - I have just written to North Bridge of your letter's arrival expecting a reply verbal, & there I mention your intent to announce in day or 2 the fixed day for your return which you to me in general terms speak of as the latter end of the month –

Marian comes ye evening to draw & she draws very well. I assure you she is remarkably improved lately the fright I believe of seeing you in the garb of criticising observation has alarmed her & worked in her the good work of reformation. Sam dear Sam is ever good & excellent - Yr Uncle Joseph is quite convalescent & I never saw your relatives more blooming & fresh –

Mrs Briggs company I was in at Mrs Weatherherd's tother day she is a pleasant woman –

You make no reply to that part of my letter where the liberality of Mr Duffin is so conspicuous, you perhaps knew of it before hand & have personally given him the large debt of praise which I owe –

Poor Miss Duffin wrote to me tother day in which letter She begs her respects to you –

I bought for 4s128Mickle's Lusiad129, a necessary work for perusal but I must say in some parts displeasingly indelicate –

Captn Weatherherd will be here in a few days.

I send you enclosed a 5£ note which will surely defray the expences of watch, the Salteen shoes, & one embossed ribbon, white embossed velvet & two or three other matters which you will remember I want – the Embossed velvet & ribbon must be narrow about ½ an inch, to go round my head as I am grown rather particular in dressing my hair –

I am too happy, fortune favors in so many ways have of late poured in on me, oh Heaven to thee I owe all of happiness I know!

Miss Philipps is so obliging that I intend her ye civility of drinking tea to meet yr family & Miss Mellin who must ask for Wednesday next –

I shall pay Darcy Hey one visit before you come home –

My nonsenses of various kinds are in number increased, a Mr Hammond of Norwich lately travelling this way with 2 or 3 gentlemen met on ye streets a young lady of colour, we'll not observe further than that he was struck with that lady, who should it be but yr very humble Servt. I am very bashful on the occasion as I learn he intends re-visiting this town soon & hopes & indeed has got the promise from a lady of introduction to me! Excuse my vanity in being pleased with such a mark from a person rather distinguished &c. however you know my long long prudence & acquired indifference to man!

{I have sent you thirty pounds & do as I desire you -} This last expression erase when you read aloud as I reckon you do as usual tho' much to our general annoyance.

Now I leave off my dear till the arrival of the expected answer from your Mother whom I don't visit today because I am so pleased with my subject of Greece my mind is totally rivetted –

While I remember let me say I have got an exceeding nice pew at the New Church lookg so respectable & tempting that yr mother means sometimes to go with me, you must ever as ye old Church can never be fit for you –

Contrary to my intention I called at N. Bridge yr Mother is better considerably & desires love &c & on yr return home you are to call at Mr Trant's & get a bottle of Mace – mind & observe the note enclosed I believe you'll find it 5£.

Write when you can my dear Sam & Marian are here & desire best love – Adieu my dearest Lister & believe me   Yr loving E. R.

130 I beg to know how you have decided about going this Evening to the concert, when I intended to accompany you & do intend if I hear anything decisive from you –

You should send to enquire after Mrs Veitch who is very ill –

Adieu my dear Friend – My kind love to Isabella –   Yrs very affect.ly E.R.

Good night my friend may sweetest slumbers close

Thy wearied eyes in undisturbed repose

May watchful angels guard thy hallowed bed

And heavenly visions float around thy head

And dreams of blissful happiness be thine

Long thought of her whom I adore be mine

Now sleep away with all thy shadowy train

For retrospection's fairy queen shall reign

'Tis she alone can every joy restore

Bid flowers revive that dyed to bloom no more

Snatch from oblivious stream dead pleasure's ghost

Teach hope to promise what we value most

'Tis she alone when sorrow's faded form

Sighs in the wind and rides upon the storm

Bids the fast starting tear forget to flow

Dries up the spring and stems the curse of woe

  Sbr. Wed. 27 1811 died

1812

Hot Wells in Bristol Mch 18 1812

Miss Lister, 1 Laura Place, Bath

I have waited anxiously ever since I left dear Bath for letter from you – which I really think you shd have sent by me to the Duffins - & as you have neglected to do it, repair the fault as much as you can by writing immediately, immediately & framing for yourself some plausible apology. I shall go tomorrow - & I do assure you my heart begins to feel rather heavy at leaving this place –

When we meet again bring good looks & good spirits - I thought you really lookg ill – let me hear from Bath soon, & mention particularly the health of my 2 dear friends, & do not forget an account of Bath Schools, for which I particularly wish!

The happy visit I paid at Bath will never be forgotten by me - & I owe much of the most pleasing gratitude to the kindness of Mrs Norcliffe to whom & the family pray remember me most affectionately.

I shall not write again to either of you until you have favoured me with a letter –

Farewell!   Yrs most affect.ly,   E.R.

Tib was currently entertaining Mariana at her home, Langton Hall.

Mrs Norcliffe had inherited her family's statutory duty as Justice of the Peace, so she had kept her maiden name on marriage and her husband called himself Norcliffe to preserve the line.

Tib was born into this wealthy, influential, matriarchal family on 9th November 1785. She was six years older than Anne and Eliza. Her elder sister Mary was now married to Dr Charles Best, who had been a pupil of Dr Hunter, Superintendent of the York Lunatic Asylum at Bootham in York. He taught him the traditional way of dealing with madness. The elderly Dr Hunter had died the previous year, so his pupil had been given the post: Dr Best was now in charge of the asylum.

But Mariana's father was a specialist in mental illness and extremely well regarded in medical circles. Dr William Belcombe should have been awarded this important post because of his far greater experience. However while he was alive Dr Hunter had insisted that the asylum was to be run by a British-trained doctor; Dr Belcombe had trained in Europe.

In fact these two doctors, Best and Belcombe, had fallen out some years before, because Dr Belcombe preferred a new system of care as practised at The Retreat, a private asylum run by the Quakers. Dr Belcombe had been physician to the Retreat since 1802, and ran it with his partner Dr Alexander Mather, who wrote about it: "*From the plan of treatment is excluded all severity of discipline.*"133

The Belcombe family included Stephen, the only son, also a doctor, and Harriet, the eldest daughter, now married to a naval officer. Of the three remaining daughters at home, Mariana was older than Louisa and Anne so she would be the next to marry. They lived at 8, Petergate, opposite the Norcliffe's town house at number 9. However professional arguments between the doctors did not stop the girls knowing each other very well.

But Eliza had her own problems. She had become friendly with a man, and now he wanted to know her better.

Halifax May 14th Wednesday 1812
134

My mind will not be easy dear Welly until I have placed on paper the subject which has this morning troubled it; the affair concerns my dear Bro'135, who if I clearly judge in this matter is surely deranged or he wd never have written me such an odd eccentric letter as I this morning received from him; certainly when a letter arrives from him my head invariably palpitates; for as strong is this profession of his heart that what may be ye result God alone knows; alas that he had not afflicted me so much as by permitting this uncertain minded man from taking a fancy to me – You shall have my first letter, his answer, & then my last reply, & pray sweetest Welly if I am the guilty tell me, point it out & let me be for once mistaken in my suspicion of the soundness of this dear Bro's mind –

My 1st letter to C.A.

Indeed my dear friend you do not deserve to have been so long neglected by me, tho' I have failed to write, I have not failed to think often of you most affectionately – Just now I am seated after the bustle & tediousness of arranging my haven for ye last month, I may really say for ye first time to enjoy quiet & peace, I am of course happy you will believe, & if perfect independence compared to the blessing of possessing 2 or 3 real friends can make a mortal happy I am.

So then, & when you next see me, you will see me only looking better & enjoying an addition of calm content: here is my cot when I shall perhaps live all my life & where I shall end my days. I wish therefore you will not fail to join in that wish – How unfortunate you are that you are obliged & so shortly to return to this Town; where you never will be so happy I am sure as alas ye other place; if you come I promise to be the best of friends to you, nor will I too much lament what cannot be averted, what indeed you say is necessity, & what will never fail to give to me both profit & pleasure –

But your society must not be indulged in too eagerly by me, I must never more act as I have done, so selfishly, nay I will consider my friend's happiness & confine your visits at my door; recollect too that now my being placed alone in the house is another cause for all the circumspection in ye World –

I have not forgotten that in your more sober hours (& ever in yr friend's estimation) I have not been sufficiently so during the past –

My friend I am hurried & you will pardon my scrawl – You will hear no more from me before we meet, if that be not prevented by some happy change in yr affairs –

My Welly is gone & I (as I always feel in her absence) am dull & lonely. She is not only ye most rational & instructive of all companions but she is ye kindest, ye tenderest & ye dearest of any I have – ah if you knew her worth as I do, you wd think that ye sacrifice of my life too poor a recompense for her past, & still continuing benefits!

In friendship I have never met with disappointment indeed my Devices there have been surpassed, this it is makes me care little for all often earthly losses. My dear friend take care of yrself – From yr sincerely affecte. Friend E.R.

Whinray you will be surprised to hear has left me, she was spoilt I believe by my professg friend Mrs Veitch & her sister.

My Bro's letter this morng.

My dear friend

From an expression in Miss Lister's last letter I suspected that our correspondence was beginning to be consider'd as either ineligible or painful to yourself; and yours of ye 9th, while it breathes ye genuine spirit of friendship, convinces me that my suspicion was well-grounded –

I shall hear from you no more until I return –

What after mature deliberation you have resolved upon must I am sure be what is most decorous & laudable: and if on opening this paper you expect to find me entreating for another epistolatory communication you do me injustice.

This is merely to say that I thank you most cordially for your letter, that I trust you will not imagine any vain, illusory hopes of happiness are ye secret cause of my unhop'd for reappearance in Halifax; that I am well; that you shall find me reasonable, & ready to testify my firm & unalterable friendship by willingly submitting to every possible deprivation, and that until June I bid you farewell from, Eliza yr faithful & affecte friend, J. Alex. –

PS The regard which Miss L has for you, you only! – duly appreciate, mine may be suspected, but hers is beyond all price, "grapple her to your soul with hooks of steel", & then you will always be what you have always been, admir'd, belov'd & respected –

I trust you will not be annoyed by this letter, but I was unwilling you shd for a moment imagine that your interdiction of further immediate intercourse had giv'n me serious uneasiness –

My reply to this letter –

My dear friend

How oddly you have replied to my last letter, which surely breathed only of kindness, & naturally expressed to you that ye return to Hx136 is now so very near I thought one more letter to you might give all ye necessary news you required of myself before our meeting & moreover coincide with that plan I had formed of writing about once in 3 weeks –

In yr letter you seem to be suspicious that I have a wish to drop our intercourse entirely & in yr postscript cruelly, indelicately say with emphasis that yr affection may be suspected, tho' Miss Lister's is above all price, as if I had ever done it, or had given you reason to think so –

How unkind you have been, & how you have evidently misconstrued those expressions of regard I have bestowed upon my poor guiltless Willy, of whom to you I have ever spoken with the utmost unreserved, & who has been & still is yr best friend –

Duly re-peruse my letter & you will find that it breathes of neither reproof, neglect nor deceit! I have been & still am & ever shall feel sincerely yr friend; yr conduct hithertoo has uniformly been too noble, too amicable to be suspected; for it I am inexpressibly grateful, nor do I ever mean to suspect it till I have some very trying proofs of its degeneracy.

Now, I say no more than that I forgive you because it is my duty, & because I love my friend; but if you only reflect upon yr last you will scarcely feel to deserve it – you pretend to remember all my remarkable expressions, don't then forget at this moment particularly to bring to mind that tone of mine, so frequently repeated to you, that whatever be yr

Errors, how great soever yr neglect I will still be yr friend, & yr forgiving friend! Farewell, I shall be glad when we meet & may you never again so much distress me. From yr sincere & grateful friend E.R.

This ends this story. I would like to linger to expatiate upon it but tis near 6 I am going to a party at Mrs Veitch's I am already too late & dearest kiss farewell! Friday morning – I sit down again during the leisure of this hour to finish my letter to you & to say further upon the above subject, that I am dubious whether I may not have misconstrued this affair, but as often we are not clear judges of our own cases, pray to set my mind at ease, judge for me, tell me exactly yr opinion; for you know from the strain, language & our dispositions & will not need to have explained the motives &c. which induced such & such expressions –

Yesterday evening our party consisted of Mr & Mrs G. Alexander, yr Aunt Anne, Mr Samuel Lister & a Miss Johnson now staying with Mrs Veitch; & the nicest girl I've seen of some time –

She is a Wakefield lady about 9 months my senior, rather consumptive, grandly inclined, with more real good sense & good reading than I have often met in women, with a sweet disposition & much personal beauty, You know I'm grand & necessarily am fastidious from having all my life had such an object to look up to as yourself – I wish to cultivate her friendship & I wish also I could contrive to get her to spend a little time with me; in short, Welly, I can imagine that Margaret Wilson of Dundee & Eli Raine & I.N. as similar characters as possible only with this sufferance that Welly is a Sun that shines brighter than any other – She stays here a few weeks; & how I long to recommend her as a wife to Mr Montagu or Captn Alexander for she is a rare bird.

Now adieu to Mary Johnson whom I like because she possesses all ye prizable qualities of ye soul & heart – Hannah Malden my next Servant is desirous to come to me upon any consideration, I have engaged her & in 3 weeks she will be here – possessing I fancy ev'ry wished for requisite –

In ye mean time I have a very nice woman who offered herself but being fore engaged she stays only till ye other's arrival –

I have had a last addition of visitors; & tell dear Isabella with my best thanks for her last kind affecte letter that I returned Mrs Greenup's call ye other day after a lapse of 3 weeks; when I was ushered into ye room ye Servant returned to say Mrs G was walked out! That is I believe per to have had a suspicion of my disaffection towards her from my [remarks] at Church last Sunday, & that on going from ye house & back … I saw this lady who we all know incredibly protests against kitchen lovers & all such demeaning employt. passing backwards & forwards before a pan I think that was boiling as if apparently to watch whether its contents were happily progressing. This odd sight delighted one still more because I believe she looked round & beheld my side, glared, & made a retreat good; I pursued my journey calmly & walked home laughing at the unfortunate discovery.

Tell Isabella I mean not to spit my spite – Isabella's like delighted one; I am heartily in her favor, always dear Welly, & and have such sympathy in her present happiness in yr society – The latter part of her letter made me laugh so excellently in … I could truly say that some genuine pleasantry had I not enjoyed of long very long.

For what is ye World to me in yr absence I appreciate with people whose courtesy obliges them to trust me well, but in real heartfelt matters, or where friendly exertion is required to aid our happiness I believe wd look another way with perfect unconcern. My books, my maths, & my letters & my own reflections are all my felicities - & I look at my Servant & think in her I have a sincere humble friend – Yet after all Welly I find that life is to be ye most happy, which is ye freest from Worldly bustle, or noisy public amusements – Truly does every wise philosopher of every age & country depict true happiness to be only found in friendship, Books, retirement &c. – Mine feeling is this 'A little peaceful home bounds all my wants & wishes, add to this my friend & book, & this happiness!'

I insist upon it that no-one sees this letter, save Isabella; for [if] I thought others heard it I shd be vexed to death to have sent it – you see how little I attend to question & answer in the letter way for I question much & you answer little; this I forgive you, because I know what a York mist must be when all is groping & engrossed –

I shall be glad when you are in ye country, because hot weather & ye smoke of a Town is oppressive …

I am now in my study – my plants at my side, Il pensoroso placed before me, the masons pudding, ye greenhouse, calmness in ye air, delightful weather, my book [-] open! Welly I feel what I never felt before! Happy, contented & grateful to God! …

for you are my best & most well known friend – thinks I to myself! I think a very good burlesque upon ye present follies; & shd like to know ye Author.

Farewell dearest from yr most sincere. {I have bought you silk stockings}

Halifax May 29th 1812 Friday morng near 10

I am disappointed in my intention of sending you a parcel by this day's coach & have postponed it till ye end of next week hearing from you that you can admit me as much time as I want –

I have ye last five days been a good deal taken up with visiting & visitors – I have been constantly to Mrs Veitch's & enjoy this nice girl's society; yesterday we took a long walk accompanied by Sam on Skircoat Moor & she was delighted. They both dined with me & ye evening concluded by ye addition of Mr Veitch to our party – To day at 3 we all dine at Northgate to commemorate Mrs L's birthday.

Tomorrow eveng I go with Shibden to Crow Nest, on Sunday again to drink tea at Mrs Veitch's.

On Saturday ye 5th of June I fully expect my Bro' will be here if not before & in regard to this man let me just pause to say Welly that you accuse me unjustly when you think me fretting unreasonably. I am not unreasonable on the subject ever, for none carried it off better. I have had enough to trouble me but if ever I have felt trouble it has been momentary & my dear Welly, is not this but nature, not to feel a little & sometimes on painful affairs is to become one of one's natural faculties, & have I not always to you, as my passing feelings have been hurt, communicated it to you – But no more excepting that I wish you Welly never to fancy I give way to grief –

Whilst I am on the plains of this remarkable soil let me say I think Mr Montagu an inconsistent & a rude Man. If I excuse him at all or think that he has one, it is that perhaps real love always acts the most inconsistently, & from its extreme timidity, involves itself into perplexities & inconsistencies. I shall hear from his friend how the matter stands; that is to say without appearing inquisitive or making the matter of consequence I shall learn from him what were the feelings that led to this conduct & what have since been his thoughts & his reasons for such strange proceedings.

My shawl I like extremely – yr parcel arrived safe & all the letters duly delivered.

I am a good deal astonished with Mrs Frances Swann's letter whenever she tells me that this summer I am to have an invitation to Red House, that the general remark is astonishment at my never going, that everyone talks of it, & thinks it unaccountable, that the friend who I professedly came to live near at Hx shd now be constantly in the family where I once was an inmate unaccompanied by me – I have received a hint of this kind from Mrs Swann & am much vexed that people shd busy themselves about me when I feel so very indifferent about such affairs of myself.

Mrs Frances moreover says that she must pay me to go; upon my comg of age, for the sake of good appearance of all parties & enlarges a good deal more. I once marked, observing this expression of yours in a late letter, "May you soon taste ye honeyed sweets of our society etc." – If you know of it, let me know, tell me the plans that are formg – how it must be received & if ye prudence & policy must oblige my to accept any invite – I shd be a little inconvenienced [written across the page: The letter left wth yr Aunt has been unopened by any since you left.] so far as this, that I must add a little to my wardrobe, that is get a few morng gowns -

I confess to you Welly that I shall feel a great deal upon such an occasion, & am again seeing the early result of my best years, where All the events of my life have taken their rise – yr being there could alone reconcile me. They will see in me perhaps an altered being, but one who from an acquired conformability to the World's ways may be better --- now than before –

My house goes on delightfully – My whole House is looking almost complete, & now I begin to understand more clearly the due arrangement of a house. My Bedroom I like better than any part of it, I will try to describe it, but we agree so well in taste that I am sure that you will be highly pleased with it – It only wants 2 complete pieces of mahogany to make it fit for ye 1st Duchess in ye land & next year I'll have them.

Frances Swann is mighty desirous that I shd immediately get 2 servants & descants upon ye propriety necessity use & appearance of ye plan - & reverts again to ye ('old time') that mischievous boys make take advantage of one Maid upon an occasion etc. She is frightened to death – Thank God I have no such fear to diminish that true fortitude of which I am possessed –

Each night as I lay in my Bed peaceful & happy I feel that I could met my Murderer with perfect calm, & could (tho' now my life is happier than ever it was) willingly resign my body to dust

 – This will be a feeling more personal when I am of age137 – I do wish to live to dispose of my fortune to my mind, & my health is extremely good, & in 6 weeks ye anxiously wished for period will be here –

I have got 'Il pensoroso' framed, this is the first selfish thing I have indulged in; & the sight of it pleases me, for tho' sometimes I appear to others melancholy I am not so in reality, it is only the calm seriousness of a happy heart, where temper glides uniform sobriety –

Dear Samuel & I often talk of you, he grows daily, hourly more manly & sensible - I am to answer for him all your interrogations which I shall do progressively –

At S. Hall, I think since you left, I have been treated more courteously, & Welly it has been observed by yr Aunt Anne that she thinks my manner to her now seems quite different, that I seem as if I felt myself an object of little consequence to them & therefore pay them no further than the courtesy of polite life. I am glad of this. She also remarked yr not seeing her ye last day but made no disagreeable comment. At Home, anarchy & confusion still exist. Yr Mother gets drunk now constantly & exposes herself sadly. Every one speaks of it of course with horror & pities the younger part of the family. Yr Father is blamed for not preventing it & keeping her at home.

She can never live over ye next Winter if she goes on in this way; & those horrid creatures the Rowes take great advantage of her wonderful regard for them. They eat & drink & go on shamefully at yr House. They are still here & likely to remain. The Liverpool jaunt I think will never take place, which I shall be rejoiced at. Various schemes are laid for a removal from home, but in my mind they are light. Captn Rowe & his wife are going I fancy sometime to Ireland, & yr Mother wants to go with them –

Sam told me ye other day a most horrid speech of Captn Rowe's concern a young lady, wishg Sam a young man to like his obscenity & such like conversation. It was the lowness of the remark, & ever since I have thought he is the lowest of the low amongst the [vilest] of mankind –

Cpt Weatherherd's heard nothing of; & in regard to Sam's going matters are just as you left them. – In July perhaps he'll get off.

Yr Aunt Lister is very kind to us all - & yr Uncle Joseph threatens if yr Mother goes drunk there today he'll turn her out of the house. They both think of you in terms highly creditable to their sense of judgement – They are very fond of you & yr Aunt Joseph speaks oftner more like a Mother of you than in ye relationship in which she stands. She has told Sam, that drunkenness is an hereditary failing on yr Mother's side, that her Sister died of it and all her relatives have been inclined to it, & Sam sees the practice to be so disgusting that really I think he can't ever bear ye sight of a liquor of any kind.

The Stilton cheese is to be used today & yr Aunt seems pleased with all that you do, & hopes you'll stay away as long as you can for she thinks you are thrown away at home. Yr poor Father I pity, & really what man would do so much – From Weighton he returned without one payment & therefore I daresay he could not remember you as he passed thro' York.

{remember welly that you send for more when you want it if I come to York my purse shall be yours & myself the source of all wants & necessities I shall send you a pair of stays & some nice cambric pocket handers} --- I have never told Frances Swann what ready money I have had to furnish with & this teazes her curiosity I believe –

I wrote as you desired to Isabella & enclosed ye letter to Essex with your alterations which I approve, and which had I had more time to have written I shd probably have thought of –

My Servant I expect in a fortnight & till she comes the girl does very well I have – Miss Johnson is fond & fine I think, & has just given me a song, & written me things &c. a girl of a vast deal of knowledge & is a charming companion for age for youth or gaiety –

The officers here are a good deal noticed, there is the hon.ble – Bertie - , a very young man, & they say clever.

My front room won't be ready of a month or two yet, so that I despair of havg my drawing room ready till August or ye end of July – Every body flatters me by admiring my house -
…

I read yesterday 3 hours Grecian history – I rise every morng before 7. I like reading, & what I like still better is that I understand things with a very ready facility – …

Mary Johnson is a good English & Scotch historian. Religion is a study thoroughly known. She draws well. Is well acquainted with Travels, speaks extremely sensibly on all English & Scottish scenery, she travelled to Scotland a good deal – She has all Modern Literature by heart & is really a solidly clever girl. Her temper is sweet & mild & yet she can say droll things, she is handsome, delicate figure, genteel – From a coincidence of many occurrences I can't help thinking she is the very Mary Johnson Mrs Montagu's flame, who my Bro' mentioned to us – It seems tho' somewhat a notion to believe –

… I am unpractised in singing & really fancy I am so in everything thus you see that Vanity is still my predominant failing; but to you loved Welly I speak as to myself.

A Brother of Mary Johnson's is expected & he is to dine at Northgate. Welly Mary Johnson is myself with only rather less life & a vast vast deal more cultivation. It is droll enough, we are never speaking, but we are going to do ye same thing … Farewell my dear Welly.

Think of me as often I do most affecty of you & live Welly in goodness, in meekness, in honor, in every good & be happy for ye sake of yr most sincere & fond Eli R

Rec'd Sat May 30 1812   Ans'd Thurs June 18th 1812
     138

Halifax. June. 12. 1812. Friday night. 139

I am not happy to defer writing to you any longer; I have hitherto done it for the sake of the long talked of parcel, but I fancy you will be anxious to hear from me, & as since the last 10 days much has occurred, I am as anxious to write you a list of all I know –

First let me tell you in brief that my house is nearly on the finish, & to my no trifling joy the front parlour is ready for the paint.

Next loved Welly my Servant's arrival I announce, a nice looking girl of 20, she havg a greater appearance of juvenility than her age declares. – She seems as if she wd suit me, I hope it anxiously, for well you know the trouble I have had in searching for these needful aids to our domestic comforts –

Welly, I go out a vast deal; that I am happy in thus passing my time I never can boast; I visit people I care little for & who on return feel as little towards me; Welly my loved

Welly you are the line, the long tried friend of my heart; in sickness & in adverse & in prosperous situations how unexampled your conduct! Think then that of you I think unceasingly, & in yr absence feel a vacuum in my happiness which nothing else earthly can supply. But I lament not, so long as I possess you living, well, & tho' far away, still happy. This separation is a trifling privation compared with the afflicting stroke of an everlasting one –

This brings to my mind with deep-felt sorrow indeed the sad state of yr favourite friend, Mrs Greenup. One of her usual complaints that seized her, she has never before been so ill, & after a suspense of a week in hope & hear, I have just this moment heard that last night she said, 'I am a dying woman, alas what will become of my 9 children; & still more afflicting is the opinion of the Physician, who says, that she cannot recover.

Poor Mrs Greenup, or rather poor Mr G who is left behind to suffer the torments of such a loss in his fireside joys - & for the sake of a large helpless young family who will require for long the tender attentions of a mother's love –

Welly this is a stroke for me, for have I not to reflect that between Mrs G and myself there has not always existed that perfect amity which every being shd feel for another – But no more of this – lament it not too much, What is, is right –

My kind friend Capt A is here he is often at my house, & I am delighted to see him looking well. I have undeceived him concerning one part of my past Conduct, when I used to tell him that a pre-engagement of my heart obliged me to decline all attentions – I cannot live to deceive, & in the explanation of this affair my mind has gained great ease – He does not abuse my Indulgencies to him, & I am sure he will ever have that nobleness & true power of soul, never to take advantage of my inexperience & good intention for when I have erred I have erred, thro' the weakness of understanding & not thro' the unsoundness of principle – I have been, & am, & must be his friend, I feel it to be so - & believe me from his society I now extract the pleasures of yr own – A sincere & an honest friend is above all price! That I may long preserve you both is my loved Welly the first prayer of Yrs E.R.

If I can send the parcel I will next week.

Capt A requests the corner to scribble on – {I have written this letter for him to see -}
   140

*   I have as your friend permission from Eliza to say that I am now as ever very mindful of the pleasurable house I have enjoyed and yet expect to enjoy in yr society, that I participate in the happiness you profess by communicating to your numerous friends at York, that I confidently look for your letter later when I tell you that E- has made a confession that my unknown dreaded [competitor] exists no more. Further I cannot certainly tell you. But is this not enough to enchant me? After what I have suffered I may well enjoy my present situation – What I have written or am to write must be seen by my friend I will therefore end that I am always yours very cordially & gratefully JA*

Despite her attempts to discourage him, and sensing her deep confusion, Captain John Alexander persisted. He pleaded that he really was in love with her. He said it had nothing to do with the fact that Eliza's twenty-first birthday, when she would inherit, would fall on July 13th and it was now June. It was mere coincidence that they had become close friends a few months before.

On the 24th June, wracked by indecision and half believing him, she wrote in desperation to Anne, who instructed her to make her intention to stay single explicit in a final meeting. Whether or not Anne was jealous, Eliza followed her advice completely, even though at their final meeting Captain Alexander seemed to her an *"uncommon, noble and truly amiable man…"*

But Captain Alexander still had no intention of giving up. He continued to try to see her at every opportunity, giving rise to gossip. He also did his utmost to convince Eliza that Anne would not keep her promise about living together. He was being honest, telling the absolute truth that neither woman wanted to hear. Eliza, shocked by this, begged Anne to tell her if this was true. But Anne, far away in York, did not reply to Eliza's question.

Instead she told Duffin selected facts about Eliza's suitor. She also informed Captain Alexander that all his letters to Eliza and her replies had been copied and sent to her guardian. Anne told him that nothing had been kept private, therefore he could not use this means of coercion. Furious, Captain Alexander went to see Duffin immediately. He stated his case clearly, but Duffin insisted that there would be no marriage. In despair he wrote a final letter to her:

"Almost horror-struck at the gloomy prospect for my future life, and acutely afflicted for the shame I have had in occasioning that anxiety and horror, … To Mr Duffin and Miss Lister I have asserted that I have had encouragement to persevere in my addresses until a late period; if this be incorrect you will pity my self-deception.

…I told my father and brother and Mrs Veitch what claims I thought I had upon you. When I see them again I shall say simply that tho' my hopes are disappointed,

my gratitude for past kindnesses and respect for your general conduct will always be yours. The same shall I say to my friends Montagu and Scone.

Understanding that you had forwarded my letters to your friends at York… was the cause of my journey. …your friends were my friends also.

I bid you Eliza heartily (can I say tenderly) farewell.

Tho' I must remain at Halifax; you know my circumstances will not admit of any other arrangement.
141

Eliza felt guilty: "…he had an unprotected faulty girl in his power, [but] could and did only exert humanity towards her, in the place of well-merited injury…"142

The effect in Halifax society of this breach of contract (though Captain Alexander did not bring it to court) was to make Eliza a pariah; she was considered too rich, too isolated, too childishly innocent, too much the wilful temptress. She was consequently "cut", shunned by Halifax society, completely ostracised by all of her former friends.

"I wish I could leave Halifax for three months, if it were not for appearance. To whom can I go?"
143

Anne meanwhile was spending the summer with the Norcliffes in luxury. Eliza was now very lonely; she reminded her partner that they had known each other for eight years, meaning that they should now be living together. But Anne was too busy discovering pastures new.

The Norcliffes had a leisurely life, getting up late, spending long periods in their rooms, occasionally riding or walking across the Yorkshire wolds. Isabella's two younger sisters were coming to marriageable age and planning to come out in Bath during the next season, so Isabella asked Anne to accompany them as their guest, and naturally she accepted.

Eliza told them she would like to come too. She had no hope any longer of friendliness or social life in Halifax. But she received no invitation. In pride and defiance she reminded Anne that she had her own money now; she did not need to depend on favours.

"It is my intention to draw 250 of the principal [assets] which will reduce my income £12.10/- a year. With this I shall clear myself, have furnished my house completely, & be enabled to make Mr Duffin a handsome present, & have in reserve for your Bath jaunt either 30 or 40 £s, and this I shall give you."
144

Both Mr Duffin and Anne objected strongly to her withdrawing assets, but Eliza was defensive. She must leave her unhappy situation. What else could she do if nobody helped her? The bills for her new household began to roll in.

"My bill at Smith's comes to £105, that at Adam's to £50, that at Farrar's to £40, that at Abbott's to £20; these different sums amount to £215. I have by me what will barely keep my house till December. I shall before then want £20 for my rent, so this is £20 more to

the sum of £215. How is this to be discharged but by a greater reduction of the principal than you propose?"145

I have now given a fair statement, and that I have been extravagant I confess. I have actually wasted £20 in furnishing, and I have bought much that is unnecessary, I find. Condemn me not. I must have from you only kindness or my heart will break. …

I have received from Coutts a Power of Attorney, which I've signed, etc. & sent up again, requesting them to discharge a small amount in respect to that, and also an Attorney's bill of £10.14.10… I have in my Banker's hands about £10 or £12, which I mean should remain there.

My will is made and I have in a legacy to Mr Duffin given £500 instead of £200. It is only a proper consideration, think how much he has done for me from childhood until now, & but for him I might have been much worse disposed of. I shall not send a copy of it till you desire me. There is a great deal of my furniture which I should take away with me when I leave. I live very cheaply & spend little on my house, I seldom drink wine…

You have done right in telling Mr Duffin so much of my affairs… Lately I met Mrs Greenup, with whom I've quite cut. In regard to borrowing at the bank here, I will not do that for they are so obstructive. Should I borrow at the York bank?"

Anne knew that Eliza had made out her will to her "*husband*" after her death. She did not object. In financial terms, if not in social, she still treated Eliza as her "*wife*". Therefore she still wrote letters for her to copy to the bank about selling stocks, advised her when to settle bills and even to dismiss her second female servant when she let her boyfriend into her room. Should Eliza hire elderly Mercy, previously the Bramley's loyal servant who lent them £80 without hope of repayment when they were in dire straits? Eliza involved Anne in all her life just as a loyal wife should.

In the aridness of Halifax society, the only place Eliza felt welcome was with Anne's family. In particular she had grown very close to Sam. He still called on her for tea. Excitedly he talked about the army, for his deferred enlistment was drawing near. Uncle Joseph had given him a gold watch, and he expected to be in Fermoy, Northern Ireland on the 10th of October, setting off on the 1st. 146

Eliza said her final goodbye to Sam; then there was nobody else to talk to. In her isolation she became depressed. She consulted Dr Paley, who noted her pallid, dejected demeanour and recommended a holiday in the South for recuperation. Delighted with his prescription, Eliza immediately wrote to Mrs Norcliffe for advice, still hoping to accompany the young women if invited. What sort of lodgings would she need? Where was the best place to stay?

Mrs Norcliffe recommended Hot Wells. Eliza would need to have a parlour and a double bedroom for herself and her maid. She did not mention her daughters, Anne or their own forthcoming trip to Bath.

Sam Lister, anxious about leaving Eliza on her own, sent her a letter announcing his arrival at Fermoy and telling her to take the news to his relatives. Liverpool had been full of confusion due to the elections, so his ship had set sail a day late, arriving on Sunday. He had been sick on board. From Dublin he had taken the mail coach to Fermoy, arriving on Monday evening. He was enthusiastic, had been to see a court-martial and was determined to avoid "*W., W. and Gambling*".

Alone, with no servant and no friends, Eliza was depressed and not eating well. She decided to pull herself together and take the initiative. At the end of October she bought a seat on the mail coach from Halifax, hired a chaise to Miss Marsh's lodging and arrived unannounced. She insisted on being taken to Bath with the Norcliffe party for the sake of her health.

Bemused and taken aback, Miss Marsh found her a bed at the Duffin's house and sent a frantic note to Anne in Langton, who came straight away to remonstrate with her impulsive friend.

Eight days later, when Anne had convinced her that she was irrational and over-emotional, and after Eliza had apologised profusely for her jealousy of Isabella, which she admitted must be due to her illness, she was sent back alone to Halifax, with promises that they would see each other when lodged in Bath.

At home Eliza went straight to the Lister's house to ask Jeremy to auction some of her furniture to speed payment of her overdue bills and fund her excursion to the south. She readjusted her will to cover debts, and rehired her first maid Grace Whinray despite her slight consumptive illness. The furniture sale was planned for November 10th but deferred for a week. When it finally took place the furniture failed to reach reserve prices and did not sell. Local people, still wary after the episode with Captain Alexander, stayed away or did not bid.

Mortified and with less money than anticipated, Eliza set off at the beginning of December.

The two-week journey was balm to her troubled mind, and lifted the strain of the past six months. Her letter to Anne on arrival detailed the stunning scenery of the Pennines, the wonderful country south of the Welsh border via beautiful Worcestershire. She was exhilarated by the strangeness of building techniques and accents. It was all foreign, new and glorious. And nobody snubbed her.

In Hot Wells the lodging proved excellent. A new routine was established. The heiress and her maid rose at 8, had breakfast at 9, sang until 10 and did English grammar till 12. In the afternoon Eliza walked till 3, then dined and read till 5. During the long winter evenings she continued her studies by candlelight with history till 7, geography till 8, and geometry till 10. For light entertainment before sleeping she read Pope's Essay on Man. It was a virtuous plan for a twenty-one-year-old woman in middling mental and physical health. She felt relief at being free of the social disapproval of the last few months and in the cheerful company of her favourite servant.

The lodgings were costly at £5 per week with £5 for sundries. This astronomical figure, a workingman's wages for a year, was twice her monthly allowance though she bought no clothing. Duffin was furious at the expenditure and demanded that she should return at once to Micklegate, since Halifax was no longer an option.

Eliza had no wish to do this. She had no more friends in either place. Anne would not live with her, just as Captain Alexander had said. It was best to look after herself.

Now she understood better what her sister had been through: a failed marriage, loss of fortune and social stigmatisation. She decided to live near her in Fulford, a different part of York. Jane was now 23 and consumptive, so she was currently in Scarborough "*for her health*". Eliza made a sensible, rational revision of her life with more emphasis on her own sister and less on high society.

She calmly informed Anne of this by letter, but Anne replied that she should steer well clear of her sister. Jane now had to work for her living and was going to find a position in Wales. Eliza, stung by this criticism of her sister, chided Anne for her "*dry, sarcastic reproach*".

Duffin wrote again urgently, demanding that she "*sink £2000*" of her capital to refund her debts, but Eliza refused. She reckoned that she could "*make [her] income do*", and estimated that she was due £400 per annum. However she had spent so much in the seven months since her twenty-first birthday that she only had £80 left for the remaining half-year. At £10 per week in Hot Wells it was plain that she would have to leave soon. But where would she go?

Sent to York by Mr Duffin Mon morng June 29. 1812
147

It needs not that I should reply at large to yr last, my time is circumscribed & as I today go to White Windows to dine & also intend havg my last interview with Capt Alexander I can have but little time for it is near 12. I will only assure you that all your suggestions shall be fully complied with. Hithertoo more perfect obedience to yr demands could not have been. I almost dread the encounter, for my mind feels big with guilt, & I know too well the wound I have made to be almost incurable. God forgive me & may he support my unfortunate friend.

Farewell! & Believe me most gratefully Yr   E. Raine

June 21. 1812
148

Friday after dinner 1812 July 24 –
149

Your letter dated York I received this morning & rejoiced did my heart feel to think, to be assured that I have 2 such firm friends in you & Isabella. Yesterday evening - Capt A – previous to his going to a dance at Mrs Pollard's called here with a letter which he told me summed up the contents 0f those 3 sheets which consisted of a history of past events which he told me he purposed shewing to Mr D.- in case of an unfavourable answer to his wishes from that quarter to prove his claims.

Never did man seem so amazed as when I told him that ev'ry letter from him with mine were sent for Mr D's perusal – This news did make him look angry beyond words can tell & disappointed too – He looked conscious that part of his conduct cd not but undergo the severest animadversion – He continued to appear very haughty, very upbraiding & I as stoutly shewed him how much I despised & hated him – & I shall still persist in refusing him admittance here, & wherever I am he shall also see that I mean henceforward to treat him as I feel towards him –

What I have still to suffer at his hands God knows only. But as long as I am saved from ruin & death – I shall praise God for his mercy. I am indeed helpless!

Of that I had some friend at my side to fight amidst this mortal warfare in my defence. But I have not even that.

Poor Miss Alexander it is said is returned from Harrogate in a state of derangement, she is under Disney's care – I pity her & indeed I pity the tormentor of my life – God preserve him from that terrible situation – I am well – But I have still greater reason than ever to think that Mrs Veitch is my most injurious enemy – The whole affair I expect thro' her means is already current

Yr stays are done at last – I hope they will fit you – Mr & Miss Briggs have called upon me.

Farewell – May you never endure those miseries which uninterruptedly prey

upon the heart of yr faithful friend   E.R.

PS Pray is it true that you have been ill? Joseph Watkinson heard of it, & brought the intelligence to Hx-

Capt A persists in refusing to take his picture & of returning my ring.

Sunday night, eight o'clock Septbr 6 1812
150

Marian has just now been here to tell me that a conveyance is at hand to avail myself of it, of forwarding a letter to you – of course you know I wd not neglect such an opportunity of pleasing myself & of giving you the dull order of my deeds – I have little new or striking to say – but to you Welly if all else were dead, affection has still a something to utter – I can forever tell you of my love for you, & tho' habit has made affection's tongue so familiar & so diffuse, it still with me is warm & prattling & fresh as ever.

I confess to you, that the oftener you are parted from me & the less I enjoy of yr society, the more do my desires increase for it; To have enjoyed yr society, to have lived so long in the tenderest hands of friendship, to have enjoyed as I have done the most exquisite sweets of your love, unfits me for any & every other object!

What makes me so cold towards the amicable, clever, & really sweet girl, Miss Johnson, whose friendship most wd deem a treasure worthy to be claimed, worthy in a high degree to be gained, but that I have been spoilt in my Welly? –

There is one substitute that I find, the only one; & 'tis well that such an one exists to soften the bitters of disappointment & absence – Books are my friends – There I see, taste, I enjoy the superiority of thought & idea which you eminently possess, & in some books I find the traces of yr noble & great heart! - But books by enlarging my mind, enlarge my wishes; I cannot read of a great thing or action, but I long to be the one, or to do the other! I never hear of nations where arts & sciences & deeds might have been done, but I long to visit each, & in remembrance act them all again, Nothing is grand, sublime nothing in short quit of the common causes of things but I am ardent to engage in it!

Now tell me, tho' Welly, much good as I may gain in one sense from books, whether this consequence from the perusal is not prejudicial? Or will you tell me, that such ambition is laudable & happy? Books have made me sick of Hx and all things in it. Tho' I know but little, yet my perception is becoming much quicker, that peoples manners, their ideas, their actions seem very insignificant & insipid - & tho' my house boasts all the comforts of life & all its tranquillity, yet my mind is not the tame thing it once used to be, to correspond with my present situation – and it seems to me, that I want society – a creature rational to whom I wd speak without disguise, & who in sharing with me the fruits of literature wd joy in each improvement & by sympathy accelerate my progress & givg an additional charm to exertion. Such a creature I want then to render me happy.

But complete happiness, they must say, was never an inhabitant of this World. I don't expect it! & therefore I mean to follow yr true philosophy – of being reconciled to every thing impracticable to our desires – yet nature sometimes rebels, & still, still Welly I feel the corruptions of humanity – They are so interwoven in our frame that they are scarcely destructible. But as Josephus says, 'Tho' Reason may not destroy our passions, it will rectify & keep them in due subjection', & Periander says 'Nothg is impossible &c' –

Welly, I write to you as my thoughts flame in my brain, if they are condemnable, condemn them only in secret, & uninteresting as they may be to you, yet since the disburdening of them on my paper is a relief to myself you will pardon the entire disguise which I throw off -

You know the source of all my serious & grave thoughts, you know what first inspired my resolution, what first gave me a taste for Books – All reason, all knowledge, any perfection that I may have in future life is to be ascribed to that source! –

If durg my earthly career, I obtain not the fondest hopes of my heart, at least that heart has taught its own improvement & the means of rendering existence tranquil & useful & even happy

I long to hear from you - & I felt much chagrined when I read in yr letter to Marian of the delay likely still to attend that letter to Capt A – it wd have been much better had it been dispatched long ago – but you have as you say ample excuse.

This mind has been on ye rack for it, & I can imagine his feelings. You may think he does not deserve mercy in any way; but W. I am inclined to think better of him. He has erred, but he has erred through his passions which havg been great & ungovernable; yet I think that there are few but wd have done worse. If I plaine him, it is at the final juncture of affairs; I think his tryg to mortify me by a total & reckless desertion & neglect of me puerile & unworthy a great mind – But I also grant that bitter is the gall of disappointment & bitter also is the idea of being an object of derision to her for whom he has so sincerely sighed –

What he does with himself I know not. He has been from Hx – but where he has been I cannot even guess. Now he is in ye E. Riding151 - Miss A still is a prisoner in ye house –

I find out that in reading only Josephus, that I feel the extreme littleness of my friend. I can scarcely by Novr gain a slight general knowledge of Asiatic Grecian, Roman & English history – When I have got this, I can then successfully pursue the regulations I sent you – to engage my mind with too many things will only perplex it, & render it still more ignorant by being still more confused. I give myself 2 years for attaining a very good notion of these several histories, of grammar, geography & Astronomy & a good chance of Belles Lettres – At ye 2 years expiration I look forward to, hope & propose leavg Hx –

I have several plans of fixing or disposing of myself which my memory will keep for yr amusement when we meet – I read only now at the rate of 5 hours, & only read Josephus – I have for 2 months gradually brought myself to bear the 5 hours steady readg without bodily suffering. I unite to this long walks a temperate diet & long sleep. & I hope soon to be able to bear a much greater exertion.

We may bring ourselves to anything: we are truly the creatures of habit - & I am anxious as so much of my life may be spent in solitude, to employ with ease everything for my amusement – To be idle a moment, breeds disquietude - & leisure is an enemy I dread –

Welly, I am not my former self. I am no more a helpless woman! No trial of suffering subdues my courage! Happy Religion! Thou hast taught me all I wish to know. In thine arms I delight to rest! Religion! Holy friend, I will never forsake thee! From my childhood until now, how oft hast thou nursed me in thine arms! How oft hast thou snatched me from the yawning gulphs of despair, of misery, & of death. Thou shalt press my age, & quiet lay me, when this earthly scene shall pass away in the icy couch of my last repose!

The cheering Pilot will steer my little ship in the tranquil seas of life; & will finally bring me to shore unto that pleasant Land, where Jehovah reigns, & where eternal sunshine gilds the blessed hours of spotless angels!

There, there & that happy shore unvarying look, & when thy soul desponds at sight of tempests & of storms rely on Religion, church & her cheery smile , & thy life shall pass away still as the last rays of setting sun! Yes my soul, thou art now as calm! Amidst all thy doubts & fears & woes, still God vouchsafes to console thee; and in thy Religion see the purest sources of present & everlasting joy.

O God! To thee I look up! Pity & defend a fatherless lonely orphan! Be thou my father & my protection, & give me, of merciful Father, when death shall take me from this world, a blessed abode in thy realm of spotless light. Amen

These are grave reflections, & I once thought of withholding them – But as they came uppermost in my mind just then, remarkably affected, I was determined my W. shd see me natural & to whom dare I be so but to you – You never criticise me maliciously – If you were to do it I cd bear it from you – … - My spirit is great – Speakg of this, the people here I believe think me a very distant & odd character! Yet to be an object of so much observation surely is flattering? I never go out of my door, but I am really so stared at & observed as is quite amazing; I never enter a room but a general silence ensues, & all eyes seem eager to remark every thing I do or say. I smile to think, that my stile of dressing, my attitudes, my smiles &c, &c, are deemed worthy of imitation - & indeed Welly I feel myself made of more consequence thro' envy detraction &c than I can tell you – I believe I improve in my manners havg gained an ease of walking & speakg not very general her, & I have got an air more of fashion than formerly. Alas for what purpose. It will never be useful to me.

My little maid Holden tells me that she never heard such a piece of work made about any one. Rich & poor, high or low make me a topic of conversation - & she seems, silly girl, to think that thereby she gains additional consequence; at least I can see this is a powerful surprise –

She is a very clever, quick girl, & if I did not think that she might be spoiled from so much notice, I wd not hesitate to make a companion of her – She sometimes hears me read poetry, for which she has a great relish & feeling, & much that she has read, both in prose too, she can repeat with a propriety & feeling not to be expected from a servant; & she seems candid, & innocent as virtue & youth ought to be – I believe she will certainly remain with me –

She has no friends but Sister's - & if she behaves well she will always find me a Mother to her –

Pray, say how Isabella goes on – Is she well, & is she not happy? Indeed the little usurping minx is very happy in you – How long she is to have your society – She will be spoilt I fear & her prosperity will make her careless & fearless of adversity – When she parts from you the pain will be more acute than if fortune had been more sparg in her indulgencies –

Isabella's philosophy is not so great as her exalted attachments, if it were her sufferings wd be less. She is a sweet creature, & I love her more sensibly for your sake – I see her the friend the partner of your future years; I see her yr most rational & tender companion; I see her the reward of every desire, & I see that she must be preserved to you for ever! God grant this my W. this is a prayer I have long uttered for you! & when I see the one bereft of the other, I shall deplore the fate that did not root the beauteous plants together – As for my Welly I shall copy the words of a great man in regard to my life –

Human life is after all a forward child that must be played with & humoured to keep it quiet till it falls asleep & then the case is over!

At one and twenty there my sentiments152 – The earlier we are wise, the fitter we are to tread the thorny regions of this nether World -

Mrs Greenup is gone to Blackpool with her charmg, enticing, & I think odious Miss Parkhill – Who is not only satirical & severe with but few pretensions to mental perfection – but whose morals I think neither refined nor fine –

In Wakefield her conduct was so notorious in respect to an Officer that many genteel people have withdrawn her acquaintance – This I hope is not true –

Every one I see I think such awkward graceless beings – This morning at church Mr Greenup struck me as being particularly so & by way of exhibiting to universal gaze his fine form he stands in such a way that I am shocked, & compare him with some that I have seen, whose delicacy I so much admire, & lament that all men are not alike – I cannot endure a masculine man –

Dear Samuel is wonderfully improved & I am extremely fond of him – You know that he is gazetted & expects to depart in a fortnight or 3 weeks if not earlier – Pray give to Mr & Mrs D my most kind love, & let me hear how they both are & what is become of the good people at Nunmonkton.

Does that sweet boy Willm still possess his enfantine graces & charms? He was a lovely babe, & nature had gifted his little heart & mind I thought richly – But education forms both – The best nature may be spoilt, & the worst improved –

Mrs Frances Swann is established by this time in her new maternal character I suppose. That is a rigid, morally good old maid. She has injured the complexion of her ways & ideas by celibacy & retirement – she means well I believe for she always writes very kindly –

Can you tell me any news of the James' & the Duffins'. I shd like to know how Mrs J manages with her large family, & when he is going - & of Miss D's how they are fixed & relish the beautiful country of Wales.

The Bramleys are all gone to London, & have embarked in some new mercantile scheme which I hope will recompense them for all past reverses of fortune.

Henry Priestley is married to that rich damsel you heard of – the bride and her spouse have been at White Windows.

At Northgate they vegetate as usual, ditto S. Hall; & ditto St Helens accord to Miss Marsh's phraseology – To that Lady remember me most kindly kind - & I shall be glad when I hear she has again returned to yr fire … – She was formed for society, to keep up the spirit & the life of all around her.

The Artistes of my drawing room have the following names – you'll exclaim how refined. Settees, Coffee Tables, Sofa Tables, Pembroke ditto, Bronze Dianas, Marble Supporters & Pyramidical Candlesticks, Venetian Blind, Turkish Cushions – How much description may exceed reality – I cd describe the beauty of this room far, far exceeding the reality – Thus much I can say, that it is chaste, genteel & comfortable –

It is a happy art to say just the reality of any thing & giving it only its true character – There is an instance within my knowledge, where the most extravagant language wd fail in describing the reality – That is in regard to you. Many have raised yr talents & all yr powers in a very exalted way, but I never knew them but very deficient of yr truth – Every one is surprised when they see you, to perceive you so much above all description –

How many cd call this flattering! But you cannot suspect me of so base & so despicable a folly. No, no, I never flatter you – I cd not even now [seek] to do it – I will never resign the charms of truth for the vices of description – There is an inward monitor that beats strong & painfully when we do evil - & my dr. W. tho' I may act ill in every other case may I never so much injure you – farewell for tonight!

Monday morng, 9 o'clock. Just breakfasted & ordered all household affairs, I am ready for nobler pursuits – First I begin by finishing my letter to you - & then I shall walk to your house with it, & return home to enjoy for great part of the day Josephus – I walk generally in the Eveng about 5 & 6 & 7 – I must conclude in haste – Believe me always

                             Yrs very affectly.   E.R.

I have had yr families to tea – They were my first visitors & in a fortnight hence I must give two Routs -
       153

Miss Lister, Micklegate, York154   Halifax, Septr 28. 1812

My Dear Welly,

You perhaps know that I wrote to Mr Duffin not long since to know what I was to do with one of my coughs which I need not explain to you.

Mr Duffin's prescription on arrival being come days after my statement to him, it was fond wd not suit me as ye symptoms had rather altered, not being so severe as at first.

I consulted Dr Paley always thinkg it best to consult ye fountain head of present advice. He gave himself a short time to understand my complaint, he did so & ye result was that he thinks ye air here too bleak & cold, & that I had better go to ye South –

So I am ordered to Clifton, & tho my darling my quarters will not be very agreeable at being so far from my Welly, I think it better to submit quietly, fearing if I do not use precaution now, I may suffer more in body than I like, or is at all needful, when I have ye ability to avoid it. I believe I must set off as soon as possible, ye Autumn being close at my heels & Winter's long scythe at hand to cut down every tender plant – I wish vastly you were here, for yr head is better than mine in … difficult situations.

I have planned ye sale of my furniture, all but my bed which I don't like to part with& indeed I need not being likely to have exclusive enough money to travel, & to get lodged at Clifton.

My spirits are very good & I almost cd smile at ye opinion of ye Doctor's but, "be merry & wise" says evry one. & prudence makes me submissive. Write to me now soon & put me upon plans, remember I must act a great deal alone at 200 miles distance.

                        Yr most fond E. Raine

I am anxious to leave Capt A a note of good wishes, don't object to ye following one –

'Change of air is thought necessary for my fallen health, I am therefore on ye point of leaving Halifax and however ye event may turn out I am anxious to leave you my best wishes that you may be well & happy in this World. And – if you think I have ever injured you in word or deed (God knows how undesignedly!) now pray forgive me, & I shall feel blessed for a real kindness conferred on yr very sincere well-wisher,

E.R.'

I shall leave with you my bed I lament parting with it nor need it be sold –

Miss Lister, Norcliffe Esq., Langton, Malton

York Novr 3d 1812

You wd hear from me by a private conveyance the other day, I have never received a reply, but shd you be meditating one, I must delay not my intended letter to ask you *some particular questions, until the arrival of it, as in my present case of circumstances I must & shall use dispatch –*

I just now told my dr Mr D. that I intend returning to Hx on Monday next for ye purpose of settling my different concerns before I leave this county for a more Southern one-

And if I make ye change Mr D thinks with me that I shd not delay, 'for delays are dangerous' & that such a change is necessary I believe I am more inclined to credit than my kind friend Mr D, who tho he allows that Hx is too cold & altogether unfit for me, wants me much to remain in York hopg his care &ye milder air of this Town might do all for me –

But I feel myself an altered being & altering daily, not indeed for ye better, & as I am delicate, tho Mr D thinks not in any danger, I have determined to go when I can do it, to give myself of those advantages of climate which I confess to you I think I materially want – And as such a change if it is to be done must be done now or never, I think indeed we all think it shd be done before Winter sets in – In such a case I shd leave York soon, & mean to do it on Monday.

I expect I shall be 2 weeks in getting arranged for my journey.

And as my finances now stand, it is also my intention to sell my furniture which I mean to do as soon as possible that I may not have ye expence of a journey into Yorkshire in April next for that purpose; nor encounter the danger of that prejudicial air …

As to you my W. I can & mean to part with you by letter amicably – I wish not to see you, a jaunt to York wd be awkward &troublesome, & just now I want to view nothing but smiling scenes. We shall meet again, when you go to Bath till then I shall only say dear W may you and dear I. be well & happy, & I desire that you take every care of yourselves &b fail not to write often to me.

My friends think me lookg better, & to be better than I am – but I am the truest judge on that point & think myself not so well, tho' I also think I shall be again my former self by Summer.

I shall leave my Will with Mr D & some letters & some of my foolish writings I shall leave in a bundle for you under Miss M's care, knowing that you will set a value upon my most worthless possessions - & in time I wd advise you burn them –

But now for the real reason of my writing – I want you to ask these questions of Mrs N[orcliffe]155 & I also request to have a very minute answer – What does Mrs N. think, a lodging at ye Hot Wells wd be taken half yearly one sitting room & a double bedded room for me & my maid –

In ye Winter & Spring I must have fires all day in each room, ye parlour for myself & ye bedroom for my girl to sit in; where she wd eat her meals also, & scarcely ever venture into ye kitchen –

I must look for ye most reasonable lodging & therefore I care not if it be a humble one, as I can afterwards improve myself if needful.

The next thing is, what wd ye board of 2 such people be? I shd only want my dinners sending up. & bread & butter. Tea wine malt liquor, groceries, linen 7 silver I shd have of my own. This is nearly all I have to ask.

Now dear W don't be long in answering to them. When I get a clear idea of ye probable expence of living at Bristol I can provide & act accordingly with frugality – Mrs N perhaps can tell you whether washing is dear – I must know all this immediately, again I call upon you not to be a procrastinator - & dear W I will thank you sincerely.

Expences calculated for being at Clifton	
Rent	50-0-0
Washg	15
Coals	8
Wine &c	5
Housekeep'g	60
	138-0-0
Cloaths	20
Wages	10
Sundries	10
	178-0-0

Sale of furniture conjectured

Draw'g room	43
Din'g d'o	14
Passage	7-3
Green Room	17-10
Bedrooms	13-0
Kitchen & Store Room &c	16-0
	11-0-13

Expence of Journey to Clifton calculated

2 people	20-
Carriage of trunks	10

The money from ye sale will be wanted for my journey & present expences being then total £92. I shall have left on arrival at Clifton to set up house this deduction £18 to last till January.

Farewell! May you always be as happy as you deserve to be – My kindest love to ye sweet girl of yr heart.

The family all beg to be particularly remembered. I wish you to present my compts to Mrs N & many thanks for ye trouble she has on my account –

I have been thinking that I might defer fixing upon my lodging till I get to Bristol – as I am yet equal to the exertion …- in that case I shd wish to know from Mrs N's friend ye *names of the most respectable houses, that I may take a survey of all & decide as I like –*

My beloved Anne, Eliza has said everything, I dare only to add a Request that you will immediately reply minutely to all her Requests – Why have you so long neglected writing to her. Don't be guilty of the like again. She feels tho' she says nothing. You possess a Heart & a Disposition incapable of voluntarily giving Pain, & ye from Inattention, you do cause it to those most fondly attached to you –

I say nothing about Eliza's immediate departure as it is settled by wiser heads than mine… My kind love to all the good family you are with – ever & ever dearest Anne believe me your fondly attached MJM

Miss M is wishful you should write to me but Welly don't imagine that I am hurt at yr silence. I am not for it is unavoidable.   E.R.

156   Halifax Novr 26th 1812 Thursday

Seated at yr Mother's table my dr W I am happy to give you as much news as I can at as early an hour as is in my power –

I am much disappointed at havg no account of Bristol, & as I shall feel but a lost & helpless creature amidst faces perfectly unknown to me I am determined to put off my journey thro' the persuasion of yr father till Monday next, hoping still in the immediate time some intelligence of consequence may reach me –

In case I do not receive that intelligence I think prudence will dictate my removal on ye Monday therefore I shall set off on that day at any rate, & if I have not written information concerning lodgings I must have recourse to verbal ones from the first person I happen to meet with, after I have called at ye door of Mrs Sixsmith & my enquiries there have proved useless –

I trust that my purse will answer all my wants. By the sale I am a considerable loser as you will see more particularly by a statement I shall tomorrow enclose in Mr Farrar's parcel to Langton, yet I think I shall have 100 pounds to pay present bills & expences at Hx, & have remaing I hope 30, or nearly 40 for my journey. In one month's time my dividends are due (in ye Stocks) & I hope to be with economy easy in my circumstances till then – you have now received all I have time to tell you about ye sale - & ye rest you shall have as I said before tomorrow –

You will require to know of my health, that is progressively amending & I expect perfect recovery in another air & amidst other friends –

Sometimes I grant a pang arrests my heart as I contemplate ye vast change now agitating, & I feel that I cannot leave Hx – without some sighs & tears but I will not interrupt your present tranquillity with ye recital of them. I hope however you will long enjoy yourself & be happy wherever you go –

I wrote to York after a delay of some days, & I received in reply from Mr D the nicest & dearest of letters – I do flatter myself that he is attached to me & this is a wealth I would not part with for kingdoms –

Miss M also wrote an anxious letter & I begin to feel some very sincere love for her & gratitude for her tenderness to me in York – I fix York in my imagination as the goal to which I shall steer at last –

My letter is a most stupid thing, but what can you expect from a stupid being, in a morning I am often lethargic & my intellect partakes largely of corporal feeling.

Whinray is grateful to you for ye remembrance & I find in her attentions most real comfort – She is a rare bird in these degenerate times, & wherever I tread my foot she will be nigh at hand to save me from harm – for she has a spirit to encounter difficulty danger & misery – Ought I not to be thankful for havg at last gained that for which I have so long wished? –

To my dr Isabella pray remember me very affectionately she is a wise & an amicable being & therefore needs but little tuition to accomplish perfection – May you long be happy & well together!!

I am at yr House & my servant at Mrs Veitch's – The solution of ye numeral proposition you shall have tomorrow I shall write to Mr Knight for it – How often ye simplest questions are found complex –

Yr mother bids me say she shall be most glad to see you & yours on the 10th - indeed I think I have now given you all the worth of my brain & till I can feel more capable of amusing adieu!

    Yrs most affectionately   E.R.

I wish you to write before Monday – with Mrs Sixsmith's direction - & on Monday morng next I shall enquire at ye office before I set off for letters –

My route will be Manchester Stone Worcester Gloucester Bristol, so says my geographical search – If you can improve upon it let me know. Farewell!

1813

Duffin's demand arrived in January 1813 when Eliza had been in Hot Wells for four weeks, but the Norcliffe party, including Anne, had not yet moved out of Yorkshire.

In November 1812 Mariana and her sisters had joined Tib and her sisters with Anne at Langton. All seven set off in Mr Norcliffe's chaise on 1st December to the Belcombe house in Petergate, where they were "*crammed into 2 beds in the same room*". Mariana went to sleep next door. The next day the Norcliffe sisters went to visit friends in Beverley for two weeks, while Anne visited the Duffins. On the 14th November 1812 Tib got back to York, then she and Anne went to Haley Hill in Halifax to say goodbye.

But Tib's only brother arrived home unexpectedly in England, having gained leave from his military duties abroad. Unwilling to miss him, Tib insisted on returning to Langton. Anne stayed in Haley Hill for the moment, returning to York three weeks later to join Tib and Mariana in Petergate where they had become "*most intimate*". After another week of preparations they were finally ready to go.

In mid-February 1813 Eliza was overjoyed to hear that Anne was finally arriving in Bath, even though she herself was getting ready to go back to York. Her own health had improved; she was now "*fat & well*". Despite the "*pleasures of walking & reading*"[157] she was feeling isolated and in need of company. She had had only one visitor, the "*ill-bred & illiterate*" Mrs Priestly, who had told her "*Coming to see you…will really be charity.*"

Miss Lister, 1 Laura Place, Bath *Mch 1813 Saturday morning*
    158

I received yr kind letter my dear Friends too late to answer it by yesterday's post - & be assured I am most happy today to write you word with what real pleasure I shall take up my above with you on Monday night next. Pray express to Mrs Norcliffe for me that I feel much flattered by her wish to see me – I am in a great hurry for I am just setting off Bristol therefore I can only say that if the Oxford mail cannot convey me out at ½ past 7 in ye morning I will travel either in ye 8 or 9 o'clock ones. The weather is rather colder than it was & I have in consequence therefore put off my journey north a week – I go on the 17th (of Mch 1813 A.L.)

Farewell!   E. Raine

Eliza was eager to see not only her friends but also Bath on her return home. She was in good spirits, looking forward to seeing the last sights near Hot Wells, and addressing both of her friends simultaneously with the name of '*Rose*'. She was pleased that they had not forgotten her, invited them to stay at her lodgings and told Anne of her intention to study with her.

Eventually Mrs Norcliffe and the young ladies set off on February 19th 1813 in Mr Norcliffe's coach and four accompanied by a chaise and pair. Together they travelled through Sheffield, Derby, Birmingham, Worcester and Rodborough, arriving a fortnight later.

"Got to Bristol a little after 11. Walked from the Bush, where we drove to the Hot Wells, a porter carrying our hat box, for which charged 2s – an imposition."

After walked along the river and thro' Clifton & returned to ER's lodgings, stepped into a Hackney coach and drove to Bristol. Saw the Blind Asylum.   159   I.N. called on Mrs H. Morris. Could not [call on] Mrs Strangeways in Berkeley Square.

Returned and got a good dinner with dear Eliza, whom we found quite well. In bed when we first arrived."
160

The Norcliffe party settled into luxurious lodgings at 1, Laura Place, Bath. Next day they began daily excursions to drink the water, preceded and followed by ritual walks through the city to parade fine clothes and other personal advantages. Every afternoon 'at me' invitations were issued or honoured, with card parties and balls every evening to enable eligible young people to meet each other.

Anne was a guest supported by her hosts, so she could not bring her own guests even if she actually wanted to do so. Eliza was never invited to stay with them in Bath, and did not have the funds or social contacts to take part herself. A few days later she decided to cut her losses and return. Now that Anne had said Fulford was out of the question she would have to go to Micklegate. She began her homeward journey on the 10th of March, accepting an invitation from Anne to stay overnight at Laura Place as she passed by.

In March 1813 Eliza told Anne about her journey back:

"In the morning met with 2 gentlemen in the coach who were extremely civil – one of them I discovered to be a Major residing in the neighbourhood of Malton in the following way: in conversation we were talking of learned ladies – he declared his aversion to them – but, he said, he had once met with one that he both admired & liked – he mentioned Miss Lister, at which my countenance expressed such joy that I believe he

fancied I knew her & asked me if I did – I told him that she was the most intimate friend that I had – upon which as you may suppose we got more intimate & agreeable –"

Waiting for Anne to return so that they could resume their life together, she made it up with Mr Duffin and began to visit people she and Anne knew. She was feeling well and happy at finding her feet in the world and acting independently. She had few people to visit since her friends still in Bath. Mariana's family, the Belcombes, were very much occupied: Doctor Belcombe and his assistant Dr Mather were opening a new private insane asylum in Clifton Green, to be run along the lines of the Quaker asylum. Inmates were to be treated with patience and kindness; they were to be offered means of recovery, rather than just being locked up for life.

Then on June 19th came catastrophic news out of the blue.

"This morning we heard that young [Samuel] Lister had got drowned in a pleasure boat. He lately entered the 84th regiment and went to Ireland. He was a young man very unfit for the army as he had very little spirit and appeared very dull, but his family encouraged him to enter it, and now I think they blame themselves very much."
161

The news rocked the family. Their Irish relatives left for Ireland immediately without taking Rebecca Lister with them. Captain Lister wailed at his wife's drunkenness; both were consumed with grief at the loss of their last son. Rebecca was especially enraged that her husband had made her son enlist.

Sam had been the only living male heir to the whole Lister family in Halifax. There was a distant branch of the family living in Wales with sons, but the Halifax Listers had been a much bigger branch, and they wanted to keep their property. Unfortunately all the other Halifax Listers were childless and elderly; only Jeremy and Rebecca had living children, and they now had no sons. Only two daughters were left, Anne and Marian, so Anne, the eldest, was now first in line to inherit.

Anne had mixed feelings: the terrible loss of a brother was balanced by the difference in their temperaments; she and Sam had never been close. Sam died in the army, but it had been such a miserable death:

"… Miss Lister has said that she would not have regretted her brother's death so much if he had died in the field of battle."
162

She returned from Bath to Shibden Hall for the funeral, and then to discuss her new future with her family. Anne did not invite Eliza to the funeral, nor to Halifax. However a few weeks later when Tib returned she visited Anne at Shibden Hall for two weeks and then both set off for Langton.

Two weeks later Anne returned home through York but did not call on Eliza. The implication was clear. Left out completely, Eliza was distraught; she had loved Sam as much as any of them. She no longer dared to hope that Anne would live with her or pay her any attention in future. She felt wronged and slighted, and she had no one to share her grief with.

In the midst of Eliza's jealousy, rage and isolation Jane Boulton unexpectedly turned up at the door of Red House. Ragged, drunk and desperate, she demanded that Mr Duffin should give her back her property, accusing him and the trustees of stealing her rightful possessions. Duffin replied irately that if the trustees told the truth Jane would not be pleased with the result. She was once again furiously banished into the night. To Eliza it seemed that both sisters were in the process of being rejected by society.

Seeing Jane being sent away with empty pockets, Eliza began to think that even Mr Duffin tolerated her only because of her money. Eliza had trusted Anne, but Anne had betrayed her; perhaps she had also trusted Mr Duffin too much? Or was he simply influenced by Miss Marsh, whose sister, Mrs Greenup, had so often upset her during her time in Halifax?

Miss Marsh was livid at Jane's accusations of theft to Mr Duffin, but she was also infuriated by Eliza's permanent residence at Red House. Eliza began to notice that invitations to Red House did not always include her. She felt an outsider, isolated from the Duffin family. She became angry and "*abrasive*" to those around her. Was she an embarrassment? Had she outstayed her welcome? In response to her moodiness Miss Marsh determined to "*cut*" her.

Months passed without a letter from Anne. Then came the ultimate insult: Anne's letter to Miss Marsh was addressed only to her, with not even a greeting to Eliza.

Eliza reacted as if stung: she sent a sharply worded letter to her former friend to complain of being totally neglected. Her letter began "*Miss Lister*", adopting a formality that had never previously existed between them. She drew attention to the money she had sent continually for some years in recognition of their mutual promise. Anne sent a cool reply, and Eliza sent an angry retort, coldly logical but riddled with inkblots caused by her bitter tears.

As usual, Anne mentioned Eliza's anger to Mr Duffin - without explaining the fundamental, logical reason for it - so that he intervened to keep the peace. He sent Eliza to stay with Lady Hoyland, a kind elderly aristocrat of limited means who lived within a day's ride of York. Here Eliza was listened to in confidence. She had time to reflect on Anne's coldness, and on which lover had been more loyal to her, Anne or Captain Alexander. She pondered her options for the future and decided on a course of action.

After sending a letter of apology to Anne, as much to placate Mr Duffin and Miss Marsh as anything else, she returned to York to find somewhere different to live. A separate lodging with a servant of her own would provide her with independence and peace. She returned to Lady Hoyland for six weeks before Christmas to let her know that her problems were resolved, and the two women parted good friends. Eliza was behaving logically.

By Christmas she had found her new dwelling, a small lodging in Blake Street with two or three rooms backing on to the house behind. Located in the middle of the city, it was entirely her own place and she would live there by herself.

1814

On 29th January 1814 Henry Boulton became Lieutenant in the Madras Army. He had used his wife's money to buy promotion.

After the festive season Anne was bored in Halifax. She missed Mariana and Isabella and the carefree elegance of York. She wrote to Lou Belcombe that she would see them in Petergate in February. Lou told Eliza, but Anne did not call at Blake Street.

In June Mariana told Eliza that Anne had invited Tib to North Bridge. Now that Anne was heir to all the Listers, her family had moved to a grand new home in Halifax. Eliza wasn't invited.

Coldly angry at Anne's betrayal, she formally requested the return of her gifts during their school days: her diamond ring, which signified their engagement, her love letters in secret code, and her picture, "*il pensoroso*". But Anne was far too busy to reply; she had all the estate affairs to learn and was starting a new, torrid affair with Mariana.

Nevertheless she wished to make amends so she invited Eliza to visit her and Tib in Halifax at the end of the summer. Unfortunately when she got there Eliza immediately fell ill. Anne soon had to return to her studies in York, so Eliza stayed at

North Bridge with Anne's relatives and Tib, who was given the task of looking after her. Eliza found her ministrations less than perfect however and told Anne in the code they still used. Eliza called it "*my alphabet*", so she probably invented it rather than Anne.

"*Sketches of I.N. in Character*"
      164

Having been since Saturday somewhat indisposed, it strikes me the more forcibly that she is a bad nurse. At first she annoys or rather distresses you by sighs & croaks & seems quite out of spirits. In a day or two she gets used to seeing you ill, recovers her spirits, knocks to the doors after her, speaks loud as usual, goes in & out quickly, comes & kisses you violently, calls you a thousand pretty names, beautys, pets, angels, lambs of heaven, sweetest loves that ever were, born [-]165, asks you a thousand questions, how you are & what you will have for instance, because you like it at other times presses you to eat a raw steak when you have hardly been able to touch anything for the last two or three days and have besides taken calomel & jalap & been sick for half a dozen hours, then if somewhat worn out, one does not answer often enough, or as she fancies kindly enough, she goes on for ages about you not liking her to do anything for you, says you are cross, etc. etc. If you seem pleased with [-]166 teazes you to death to know if you [-]ally167 pleased with one from her. If ever you speak affectionately of anyone teazes you to make you say you like her ten thousand times better and indeed better than all the world.

She is curious to a pestiferous degree: whenever she comes into the room she is never easy till she has found out all you have said or done in her absence, and if she fancies conversation stops on her entrance she always thinks you have been speaking against her and plagues your life out till you have satisfied her either with a fortunate truth or a happy deceit. She sees me write this, has asked me a hundred questions, what it is about, says she hates me to write anything she does not know, that it is horrible, for she always suspects it is against her & has made me and has made me say over and over again that it is not about her or Mariana.

She has just through my sister's blindness contrived with great bungling to win a game at draughts, but at this like most other things I really think her a noodle.

She sometimes asks very silly questions about Dieppe custom house duties etc. and constantly tells one what she would advise one to do & what she would do herself under such & such circumstances & her [-] 168 are by no means inestimable, her curiosity to know what I am writing increases & she declares she will get !!!169 to teach her my alphabet.

Every now & then we amuse the party by differing in opinion about Drs Belcombe & Best.

Her conduct to my mother is anything but judicious; she orders John, prys into everything, lets Betty hear her. My Mother's in a devil of a temper, is a nasty devil etc. etc.

She has been at church one afternoon since she came here; has often, or several times drunk eight glasses of wine; gets into raptures when people are present; declares she will gobble me up etc. etc. If I don't speak often enough, however I may be engaged, says I take no notice of her, etc. etc. But no more & so much for my true observations this evening.

Tuesday 30th Augst 1814.

(Marked Raspberry Lyme Sugar Augt 1814)

She sometimes makes much of me before Marian that the poor girl wonders & asks if Mariana ever does so, tis a joke among the family. She cannot leave me a minute; I never can say a word to any of them to themselves for she is certain to hunt us out – 30th Augst.

For want of sufficient resources & sufficient exertion she is often idle & consequently has very unequal spirits, is frequently low & unhappy & sighs as deeply from ennui as any other person could do from real calamity.

I pity such a character with all my spirit.   Thurs. 6 o'clock 1st Sept. - 1814

Eliza still saw the Lister family as her own, despite Anne openly declaring they would not live together now.

She returned to York as soon as she recovered. Though still thin and haggard she was better off than her sister, a thin, consumptive, often raucously drunk prostitute.

Then one night Jane unexpectedly turned up at Eliza's lodgings in Blake Street.

"… the 23rd August. On that memorable day at nine o'clock at night a woman called at my lodgings, being out of Micklegate bar, with my unfortunate sister who desired to be admitted upstairs. As usual this request I refused.

When my maid assured me she was a sad spectacle & if I saw her I should consider it wrong to turn her from my door, prevailed on by my maid, I desired my sister to be shewn upstairs.

…I was immediately convinced by the strangeness of her dress & the incoherency of her language & manner that she was deranged. …I felt …urged …to do all I could for her protection & future safety.

I told her if she would place herself under my protection I would find her an asylum for the rest of her life.

She readily consented to my offer and she remained with me a week during which time I had opportunities of hearing confirmed my suspicions respecting the disorder of her senses."

Eliza felt an unwelcome burden to Duffin and Miss Marsh, who now wanted her to live independently. She did not go to them for help. In any case they always turned Jane away and encouraged her to do the same. Now that they were adults with their own fortunes she and her sister were increasingly isolated and in danger. They faced identical problems: pressure from bad suitors, social prejudice and ostracisation.

Mr Duffin was no longer interested in them. Eliza was lucky because she had been well looked after during her recent illness, but Jane also needed warmth and security, a roof over her head, medical care. Above all she needed a place of peace and safety where she could be taught how to live again.

Eliza had planned to share her money with Anne, but she no longer wanted it or her. From now on it would be best to share with her sister, who needed it more. During their week together, as Jane swore, coughed, ate hungrily, shouted and wept, Eliza thought of a solution to guarantee Jane's protection and continued contact with each other. Eliza decided to withdraw Jane from the world that was killing her.

"I therefore wrote to Mr D[uffin] merely for a direction to Mr & Mrs James who I knew were in London. When I had obtained this I wrote to the James' mentioning my sister's unfortunate visit & my wish to go to London to consult the first advice in case of insanity before I should place her in what I considered had become necessary, in a mad-house, & I begged of them to enquire for me who was the most eminent physician in London. I received a very kind letter from Mr & Mrs James offering me every assistance.

…Some days after my arrival thru' the advice of Mr James[170] & that of a friend of his, a physician to the Middlesex hospital, I was recommended to consult Dr Munro. As soon as it could be accomplished Dr Munro attended my sister & after seeing her a few times he informed me that from what he had heard her say & knew of her manner he felt himself authorised to give a certificate of commitment to any house for lunatics as any of her friends judged proper to place her.

…wishing to gain the acquiescence of her trustees, I sent for Mr Dickenson, the one [171] appointed by Mrs Boulton to her property. ….Mr D[uffin] …acknowledged I …was justifiable on the steps I had taken to secure my sister for the future, but that as he pitied her situation & had ever considered that the desertion & ill usage she had met with had compelled her to the commission of most faults of which she was accused, he wished before any such step should be taken as confining her for life, she should be permitted to have her liberty for six months as a trial, and if she violated her promise to be steady after this, that he would certainly comply with my wish of putting Dr Munro's certificate into execution.

Mr Dickenson then took my sister away with him, placed her in lodgings near him, promising to look after her in future."
[172]

Eliza had acted very rationally, consulting Mr Dickenson from Coutts bank where her fortune was held, and, through him, doctors known for treating lunatics. But why had she consulted so far afield? She and Jane had always had close contact with doctors. Their own father and Mr Duffin were army surgeons and authorities on public health. Tib's brother-in-law Dr Best was in charge of York asylum. Mariana's father, Dr Belcombe had a private lunatic asylum there. Why did she not get in touch with them about Jane?

Eliza was probably worried about how they would be dealt with in York; she almost certainly felt they would be treated more fairly in London. She probably also had doubts about the treatment available in York lunatic asylums in the light of recent events. In addition she was now an adult with her own means and could act for herself – and no one seemed to care about her or her sister.

The governor of York Lunatic Asylum was Dr Best, Mariana's brother-in-law. He had always followed old Dr Hunter's methods of care for lunatics. But Samuel Tuke, owner of the Quaker Retreat Asylum, also in York, had recently exposed conditions there. Tuke had engaged a solicitor, Jonathan Gray, and together they had broadcast the terrible conditions under which most patients were kept, chained to the wall, virtually or completely naked in unheated rooms with straw for bedding. Consequently Dr Best was publicly humiliated and forced to change his methods. By 1815 his health had broken down; he was forced to leave his post and escape with his wife Mary and children to Italy.

In York Dr Best's public asylum was recognised to be badly run while the father of Anne's friend Mariana, Dr Belcombe, managed the respected Quaker Retreat. Eliza wanted Jane to be kept privately and London seemed better; Eliza's bank representative, Mr Dickenson, was in London. They were sisters and Eliza wanted to use her money for her sister's benefit. She did her best to act responsibly by consulting professionals for advice regarding Jane, who seemed calmer, and who remained at her sister's lodgings despite the fact that she could have run away.

Whatever Eliza's motives, they were strongly doubted. A month later, on 24th September 1814 Miss Marsh described developments to Anne.

"… Mr Duffin last night received a letter from Mr Dickenson as to his concurrence to confine Jane, who had been …quite drunk, had got money from Coutt's bank, & in short had acted so strangely that Dr Munro had given his affidavit that she is mad. She has run away… but Dr Munro has asked Mr D[uffin]'s leave, when they catch her again, to place her in a house of confinement at £100 a year.

Mr D[uffin] is gone to York with his answer to Mr D[ickenson], which he read to me, saying that everything must be done in the most lenient & kind manner, & that as he is on the [Medical Board] Mr D[uffin] leaves it to him to take care she is properly placed till she recovers from her dreadful situation. Mr D[uffin] thinks with me she is more vicious than bad; whichever is the disease, confinement is equally necessary."

However Miss Marsh was appalled by Eliza's attempt to put her sister into a madhouse. She attempted no understanding of what Eliza was trying to achieve:

"Not a word said by Mr Dickenson of Miss Raine, a proof she has not appeared at Coutts or at Woodford with her. Perhaps Jane ran away from her, & where this poor deluded Eliza is, no one knows. As she asked Mr Duffin in a note the direction to the James' Mr D thinks she might be gone there.

She has acted in this affair completely by herself. Therefore let the issue be what it will, she has none to blame or thank but herself. Perhaps she could not turn her back the night she arrived, but to undertake to go away with her without consulting anyone is most strange; I think with you that Eliza is a little in the same way as Jane. "

Miss Marsh had no faith in Eliza and seemed to impute Jane's wild actions to her younger sister, in whom she could find only bad motives.

Miss Marsh (Red House) to Anne Lister (North Bridge)173

Your very kind and affectionate Letter my dear Anne was most welcome to me & afforded me great Comfort; in the first place to find you are so stout again … as to give every hope of a permanent recovery, in short that everything is going on as well as your best friend can wish.

I have much to say on the subject of Miss Raine but shall first answer all of your other questions.

I went to the balloon ascent and was much gratified. I also saw dear Mariana looking uncommonly well, intending after the balloon to go to the Race & then to the Rooms. She had not then determined upon her Derbyshire visit.

Poor Eliza looking dreadful, having just recovered from a dangerous illness.

I saw all the dear Norcliffes … Mrs Norcliffe was kind enough to want me to go to Langton this week. I told Mrs N. I would postpone until Mr Duffin's return; his resolution to go was rather sudden … I have been very anxious about the Asylum business …

I think all has gone off very well for Dr Best as second physician & 300 a year salary. I long for Mary's note tonight to reveal his sentiments.

Mrs Green always enquires after you. Mariana has been to supper at Acomb …

Now I have told you everything I shall begin with the curious history of Miss Raine which I did not think of our telling you, wishing not to injure her; but as you have so candidly given me your opinion of her, and as I can never mean to speak to her again, I think I should but betray you with the friendship I profess, did I keep you in the Dark.

She has been gone from Home three weeks tomorrow.

For the first week nothing could make themselves so agreeable. I was sorry to see her so little fond of reading & become a sort of tigress in conversation; then I remarked to Mr Duffin & said the loss of your society was, I thought, the cause of it. We had many discussions & when I differed from her she really was so exceptionally rude in her expressions that I passed it over the first time, the rest upon a very shy, hot occurrence. About my sister she really went on so unfavourably & readily that I said nothing. I was extremely shy with her. I never spoke but when I could not avoid it. This was on the Thursday & we were on barely civil terms.

On Saturday Mrs C(rompton) came to ask me to ride with her to Acomb to call upon Mrs Green. Eliza was in her room dressing (which generally took up many hours in the day). I called at her door to say Mrs C was here & we were going in ten minutes. During Miss Raine's absence Mrs C said, "My husband & I wish you would come to us; it is a good opportunity for Miss Raine is here." I immediately said I would and fixed the next day, Sunday, to stay till Wednesday when they were going to York. They had before asked Eliza to go there when she left Red House.

Eliza came in before we set off. The subject was not again mentioned, nor did Mr or Mrs D say anything about it whilst I was away. After dinner I said to Mr D, "You will have no objection, Sir, to go to Church at Nunmonkton, as my visit will be so short that I wish to go there early tomorrow." This was a deadly surprise to Miss Raine; she turned most black upon it. The next morning she was dressed most smart to attend, when lo! the rain prevented our going, which I really was not sorry for. The evening brightened up & Mr D said he would go with me to the river's edge; I said, "Eliza, as Mrs D does not intend to go over yon river, you won't go?" (as she never could walk in an evening, it fatigued her so much …) She said no, she should not go, and when I put out my hand she did not choose to shake hands. I said "Do as you like!" Mr D took it as a joke, and as I did not wish to injure Eliza in his opinion I let it pass, nor ever made any comments on her behaviour to me, to him or any other human being. All this I have been so circumstantial to prove to you I had nothing to do with her strange flight from here.

On Friday evening Mr D walked over to invite the Cromptons to a harness of venison. I asked why Eliza had not come; he said he never told her. I also asked privately how all went on; he said exceeding well, Eliza … was in very good spirits.

On his return, upon mentioning to Mrs D that he had been at Cromptons, Eliza said "I wish, Sir, you had told me" and he said "Why, Eliza, had you anything to send? – I did not even tell Mrs D." She said "I would have sent my best regards to Mrs Crompton." "Look", he said, "If that was all, I never carry messages." She asked if she was enquired after; Mr D said "Yes, all evening …"

At night Eliza very formally wished him good night, the same formal salutation in the morning which continued all day. After dinner she said to Mrs D "If you have any commands to York I am going tomorrow" at which they were all thunderstruck & begged she would not think of leaving them. She said she feared she had stayed too long. Mr D said nonsense; if you had stayed ten times as long they were always glad to have her. She said she expected she had. Mr D then hastily said "If that is the case, Eliza, the sooner you go the better!"

But I should have told you; when Mrs D was at home, Mrs C said "Our visit to York is postponed; therefore we shall not let you have Miss Raine till Saturday." The butcher on Wednesday evening brought Eliza a large quantity of clean cloaths & by him she sent for a chaise the next day.

Judge of our surprise when Mrs Crompton on Wednesday evening served a note to say she was going to York the next day, and would pay Miss R a visit any time she would appoint! I could not think what had happened.

The last thing that occurred was a fracas with Mr D. I desired Mrs C to us the next day instead of going to York, & I would return to Mr D. This she did; and a note came to say she could not, that she was invited to Red House for a fortnight and she had outstaid her time, hoping to visit at Nunmonkton, but as I staid so much longer she would on no account shorten her visit, & a great deal more nonsense.

I also wrote a note to Mr D to beg he would talk to her & prevent her doing what she might long regret. He wrote me back that she had taken some foolish whim in her head & she might follow her own way.

Mrs C and I walked over here soon after ten on Thursday. Mr D was gone out to avoid her. Presently she entered & very calmly bid Mrs Crompton adieu & said she hoped she had not inconvenienced her. Mrs C said how could that be; she hoped she should see her when she next came to Red House. She then took leave of Mrs D & after searching all the gardens etc. for Mr D, set off with her baggage leaving a message for him. He came in soon after & said nothing, but I saw he was very angry.

I really pitied this poor unfortunate girl & at four the next day I wrote to her saying everything that had passed between her & myself was now gone from my mind, and I exhorted her to write to Mr D and let everything be made up between them before anyone knew. In short I said everything that affection & kindness dictate and told her that no-one did or should know of my letter or anything that had passed.

I received the next day the most violent letter that ever was penned, saying she had done nothing wrong & that she had no doubt Mr D would call on her, when she would shake hands with him but only be upon passing terms. With the haughtiness and impertinence of it, she plainly perceived I had impressed Mr D with a wrong impression of her heart, faulted her in wanting to throw all the blame of her conduct upon me.

I shall drop the latter forever instantly. She sent a pair of gloves for Mrs D, and a day or two afterwards sent a pair to Mrs C with "Miss Raine hopes Mrs C will do her the honor to accept the accompanying." – Mrs C was quite vexed. She is, I think, deranged.

Mr D has never called upon her, nor will he say anything – nor don't you to anyone except Mariana, who I longed to tell when I saw her. I think the dear Isabel would take such a dislike to her for all this that for her sake one would not expose her; but you know best.

She has quite shut herself up in York, no-one sees her; what a miserable wretch she must be. I request you do not write to her upon this, or ever let her know. You know it; she deserves nothing from you, who does behave with the blackest ingratitude.

My Lady has taken no notice of her nor even invited her all summer; I think this has singedher & made the black blood to boil.

*However, I have got forever quit of the Rubbish, even to speak to. I feel vexed that I have always been so much her friend, but I wished you & her to be on good terms for her sake."*174

Having completely withdrawn herself from blatant criticism by Miss Marsh and a refusal to hear her point of view by Mr Duffin, Eliza felt that Anne must intervene. She therefore wrote a letter describing the events dispassionately and asking for her help.

To Miss Lister, North Bridge, Halifax   York, Blake Street, Oct 6th 1814

My dear Miss Lister,

It is now some time since we have had any correspondence; the fault is yours as to the best of my recollection you are in my debt. I do not however consider this of any consequence & as I have at present a subject of some moment to communicate to you, shall study only my wish to inform you of it. For the last two weeks I have had my mind & heart wholly taken up & in a way unpalatable to the former & mournful to the greatest degree to the latter.

Without any further preliminary I shall relate to you the particulars that have happened since the 23d of August. On that memorable day at nine o'clock at night a woman called at my lodgings, being out of Micklegate bar, with my unfortunate Sister who desired to be admitted upstairs. As usual this request I refused. When my maid assured me she was a sad spectacle & if I saw her I should consider it wrong to turn her from my door – prevailed on by maid – I desired my Sister to be shewn upstairs. On seeing her enter the room I was in I was immediately convinced by the strangeness of her dress & the incoherency of her language that she was deranged.

When such appeared to be the state of my poor Sister's mind I felt within a monitor that urged me to do all I could for her protection and future safety. I told her if she would place herself under my protection I would find her an asylum for the rest of her life. She readily consented to my offer and she remained with me a week during which time I had opportunity of hearing confirmed my suspicions respecting the disorder of her senses.

Having left Red House this summer at variance with Miss Marsh who has used me maliciously & unjustly I did not expect, had I made the application, that Mr Duffin would have rendered any assistance in my difficult situation with my Sister. Indeed to tell the truth my pride would not suffer me to ask a favour of Mr Duffin as of late he has made me feel the obligation I am under to him.

I therefore wrote to Mr D merely for a direction to Mr & Mrs James who I knew were in London. When I had obtained this I wrote to the James mentioning my Sister's unfortunate visit & my wish to go to London to consult the first advice in case of insanity before I should place her in what I considered had become necessary, in a mad-house & I begged of them to enquire for me who was the most eminent physician in London.

I received a very kind letter from Mr & Mrs James offering me every assistance.

After this I took my Sister under my care & left York in one of the coaches. On my arrival in London I drove to the James' in Charlotte St. They refused seeing my Sister & directed me to my lodgings which were only a few doors from their own house.

Some days after my arrival thru' the advice of Mr James & that of a Friend of his, a physician to the Middlesex hospital, I was recommended to consult Dr Munro.

As soon as it could be accomplished Dr Munro attended my Sister & after seeing her a few times he informed me that from what he had heard her say & knew of her manner he felt himself authorised to give a certificate of commitment to any house for lunatics as any of her Friends judged proper to place her.

After receiving the opinion of Dr Munro it was my intention to put my poor Sister into one of the houses for the unfortunate belonging to Dr M, but wishing to gain the acquiescence of her trustees I sent for Mr Dickinson, the one appointed by Mrs Boulton to her property.

When I saw Mr D I told him of my Sister's visit to me at York, of the motive of my accompanying her to London & hoped to have his consent to confining her to a private house for insane. Mr D replied to this that he acknowledged I had a right to complain & was justifiable on the steps I had taken to secure my Sister for the future, but that as he pitied her situation & had ever considered that the desertion and ill usage she had met with had compelled her to the commission of most faults of which she was accused, he wished before any such step should be taken as confining her for life she should be permitted to have her liberty for six months as a trial and if she violated her promise to be steady after this that he would certainly comply with my wish of putting Dr Munro's certificate into execution.

Mr Dickenson then took my Sister away with him, placed her in lodgings near him promising to look after her in future. Thus my dear Lister my visit to London terminated – a melancholy and trying one God knows.

Mr & Mrs James wished me to accompany them to the sea-side where they were going soon but I declined their invitation & returned to York on the 23rd of September & have written you the particulars as soon as I had summoned resolution.

I hope you will answer my letter soon & mention how you are. I should like in my next to ask you a particular question concerning myself.

Believe me very affectionate, Eliza Raine

Meanwhile Miss Marsh's bad opinion of her was worsening, partly due to jealousy of Eliza's affluence and independent behaviour in contrast to her own financial dependence. Her pronounced racism led her to see Eliza's actions in the worst possible light. She became vociferous to everyone in her condemnation of her and utterly devoid of any understanding of her motives since they no longer communicated with one another.

*Miss Lister, Jeremy Lister's Esq., Halifax   Red House Oct. ye 16th
1814*

My beloved Friend,

Your last Letter shocked & surprised me more than I can express as I had hoped the dear Mariana had been with you at Halifax –

I was so hurt that I immediately wrote to the dear Girl (Mariana) & had directly a most comfortable answer with Regard to her Health & as I have not had occular Demonstration that what I told to be not the truth, the whole truth & nothing but the truth I hasten to communicate the joyful Intelligence to you my dear Anne, whose Heart & Feelings seemed quite overpowered with Anxiety & Dread of what I trust & hope is as far from Mariana as any of Us –

know then my dear Welly that this sweet Girl made her appearance here soon after 4 yesterday, She (and a very sweet little Girl whose Name I never heard, being absorbed by Mariana) came in their Gig driven by a Servant, She had dined at home & meant to be here before 3 but they mistook their Road 2 or 3 times & at last got safe here coming by the Moor & the Deightons –

the Consequence was She could only Stay half an hour, nor could we visit her to do more for fear of the Dry Air, as it was I fear it was rather late before they would reach home, but the Afternoon was mild & she was well wrapped up –

It was the first Day of her walking without a Stick but She looked better than I have seen her for some time. Mrs D is quite of my opinion & was astonished with her appearance – She was in excellent Spirits & told me She was gaining ground as fast as She had lost it – of Course She is much thinner for which She is no worse – In Completion looks & hair, her Eyes look well & in short I cannot say too much of my Joy & Surprise at finding her as She is –

She is to set off to Scarbro' tomorrow & I have no Doubt of her returning hearty & robust – therefore set your good Heart at Rest about this interesting Creature as there is now not the smallest Cause for Harm. How very kind & like herself to come here, I am most pleased with it & Mr D received her so very warmly, affectionately; I may say I was quite delighted, he kissed her again & again & he shewed the Delight he felt at seeing her so very much better than he expected –he had desired me to invite her here for a Day or as long as She could – which Note passed her on the Road yesterday – Mrs D thinks She never saw her look so well – will all this satisfy you? – what a sick house they have had – poor Lou will I hope be able to follow with Mrs B tomorrow Sennight –

And now Adieu to this dear, interesting Subject and let me take up what can afford neither of us much Pleasure. Such a History as Mariana gave me of Eliza Raine has really shocked me; you will know that She wrote to Mariana and that they, like good Christians, have forgot or rather forgiven the Past & have again found themselves her true Friends.

She asked Mrs Belcombe's Pardon for her past Conduct - indeed Mariana told her it was their Intention never to notice her any more. She also gave her some Advice about you & her base Conduct to you, all which she confessed & seemed the most humble Penitent.

In short, her wretched Appearance (for she has lived upon Water for some time) & her friendship for low Conditions worked upon their Feelings & good Hearts, & they have done all in their Power to represent her Conduct in the best Light - for such Reports has got about that her Character was at Stake & her Respectability quite gone - no Creature went near her for 3 Weeks since her Return – now Julia has called, the Stainforths, etc., all which she is obliged to the Belcombes for –

Oh, Eliza, if you have a Heart to feel what must be your Sensations now towards a Family to whom you have conducted yourself with the basest & blackest Ingratitude -

I really am so shocked with all the horrid things which are said of this poor unfortunate Girl that I am ready (once again) to offer her all the Services in my Power & as the first Plan of doing her Good will be to ask her to dine with me & Mr & Mrs & Miss Duffin, I am ready to do it & shall be glad to see her - but after her Letter to me I cannot write to her, therefore my dear Girl, through you shall this Act of Kindness pass, and she can then write me a Note to say whether she will accept or not.

She may be afraid of the Past being obliterated from Mr & Mrs Duffin, and I think it will be the best Plan for her to get over the first Meeting with them, & then in Gest I will do away as much as possible the bad Impression all seem to have of her - I know her wretched temper is so vile that too much Kindness she will spurn at, therefore I have you to negotiate at the same time, making her fully acquainted that the dreadful Reports about her have raised my Compassion & Pity, which otherwise I believe would have lain dormant for Life; that you need not tell her, but that to save a fellow Christian from sinking I am ready & willing to hold out a helping Hand – your Letter to her was excellent & highly approved by Mr Duffin who pities & feels for her.

If my Lady was again to notice her [it seems] to me that she would not again treat the Belcombes, you & me as Family.

Pride is & will be her Ruin; she cannot bear Prosperity, & God knows she has had a sufficient Portion of Adversity to last her Life.

Mr Duffin had another Letter from Mr Dickinson last night, saying so far Mrs Boulton175 goes on very well at Woodford; an apothecary has attended her & declares she has no Madness about her, & Mr Duffin says he knows no such Want of Heart as in Miss Raine, who would have locked her up for Life, for no other or better Reason but to prevent her annoying her again at York. He says She had no other Feeling for her sister's Situation, but She need not be afraid of being troubled by her again, as Jane knows her sister's wicked Intentions & will never again trouble her – Mr Duffin will write to him to approve of her not being put into Confinement.

I am firmly of the Opinion that Eliza's chief Motive in all her clandestine Proceedings with this wretched Sister was to keep her from York – Pride again. Since She came home Mr D received a note from her to ask him if he knew anything of the Widow of James Raine of Scarbro' not saying one Word of her Journey or any thing else –

don't you think She is of the two Sisters the most deranged –

we return to York on Wednesday the 2d of Novr. so you will tell Eliza the day & recount the Message as you think best & the most proper, making Use of my Name as you like, kindly or otherwise; I leave all to you.

Mariana told me Mrs Belcombe or she had written to you to come to this poor Creature, as the best Mode of duping her up; you will indeed be an Angel if you do - & as Self always operates I shall see you & of Course you will give Mr & Mrs Duffin the Meeting on the 2nd - What delight but I dare scarce hope it – then we might go to Langton together – I have not heard a syllable since dear Isabel's arrival – but I mean to go there the 1st or 2ns week in Novr. …

I had a delightful Letter from Winterton yesterday, they are all prosperous & gay, nothing but gay Company & paying Visits –

many kind Wishes are sent to you & Isabel who they think is still with you - … - The Grieves & Marshes & Gorleys are always pleased with your Remembrance & they turn theirs – the Cromptons have been at the Dealys & my Lady's, I have not seen them since their Return – Gilbert Samuel did the Duty very well –

you will be glad to hear poor Tom Telford is safely arrived at his Father's home – Kent, his Cousin, came down in a Yacht for him & the Voyage has done him good – he got there about 3 Weeks ago –

Mr & Mrs D delighted at the idea you will pass some time here next year – Mr D's overt Countenance brightens up whenever it is mentioned, he will ill brook a Disappointment –

I think if dear Isabel had been very ill Tom would have written to me, it is nothing but parting from you, She will never be right without you - …

Lady Crawfurd is to dine here on Wednesday on her Road from Scarbro176' where she has heard strange Histories of Jane B. I don't know that I was ever in a Room with her. I rather enjoy the Thoughts of such a Curiosity …Remember me to all at home & to your Aunt, also I hope She has secured Benefit from Harrogate – if Mrs N is still in your neighbourhood don't forget me

My very dear & amiable Friend your sincerely attached & most truly affectionate MJM(arsh)

Miss Lister, Jeremy Lister's Esq., Halifax   19th Oct 1814
          177

You will be very much astonished my beloved friend to receive another letter from me tomorrow Morning … I must tax your Pocket again without loss of time to unsay everything kind I had desired you in my last to tell that wretched creature Miss Raine; & if your kind Heart has written to her to Day in order to give her what we thought Comfort, I must beg you instantly upon the receipt of this to do it all away, as she shall never enter my Doors again so long as she or I shall live.

You shall now hear what I am almost shocked to relate.

Mr D went to York yesterday & took your Letter. When very near returning, Betty178 came in to say Miss Raine was at the Door & asked to see him. He desired her to walk in, his good Heart feeling Nothing but Pity from the wretched account Mariana had given us of the horrible histories about her, & supposing she was full of Contrition & Sorrow for her past Conduct, he saluted her & begged her to sit down, which she did.

Nothing dismay'd and with bold Effrontery [she] began accusing him in every Way, first by abusing me & making me blacker than a D   179 ; that I had influenced him & he had joined me in setting everyone against her;

in Short she detested me & my Character (which She almost took away); that she had long ceased to respect him, she looked upon him as a great Hypocrite & had for some years stifled her Resentment for Us both; she knew I had hated & perverted her for many Years; that I had set them against her; that Mr D had joined in prejudicing Mrs Crompton; that Miss Stainforth & Miss Hall were both shy with her, all owing to me – tho' I have seen neither since she left Red House - & many other Accusations equally unjust & untrue!

Mr D says he was very near breaking out once or twice; however he determined to be cool and hear her to the End.

When he asked her to give him some Proofs of all she had said, she said she had many & mentioned some idle Nonsenses of Conversations.

When Mr D said "Are these all you have to bring forward?" upon this she rose, wishing him good Morning & giving him to understand she had done with him forever. He mildly said "Eliza, you are acting an idle, foolish Part which I think you will soon repent of" & off she went –

By the by, she told one famous L180 by saying she was making Visits as all her Friends had been most kind to her & she had no Doubt of living with Respectability; now we hear from Mariana that not a Creature had noticed her, & but for them, most likely no-one would.

She is again set up, you see, with the Morsel of Prosperity! I care not what she says of me, but to go coolly & attack Mr D in the Manner she has done proves her to have what I long thought she possessed, a malignant, black & bad Heart.

Mr D says there was no appearance of Derangement, he told Mrs Duffin he was sorry to see so malicious a Disposition in any One.

But he has now done with her forever & he desired me to write to you to Day to prevent you giving any kind Message from me to her as he says she is undeserving of any thing of the kind. Yet he desired me not to tell People of her Conduct to him as he was well aware it would prejudice them against her & he was unwilling to do her an Injury.

I have nothing to reproach myself with but having been too kind to her & you have such Weight with me that you can persuade me almost to any thing … I pity & forgive her to myself but to Mr D I neither can nor ever will –

her Conduct is the base, black Ingratitude of a Child to an excellent indulgent Parent, whose Kindness to her from her Infancy has been without Bounds. & his Indulgence unparalleled - as you ask I forgive such Conduct - none but you can bring her back to a proper Sense of her Duty & save a Soul from Perdition but even in this Case I despair of your Powers.

Much more she said about me, I am convinced … I would have her be aware in Nature what Liberties she allows her Tongue with my Character, or I may bring her to a Court of

Justice – not that I think for a Moment that she dared do it to any One, but I shall soon be informed when at York – for after daring to attack Mr D what dare she not do –

I dare say she is now thinking she acted the Part of a great Heroine - I believe if she met me she would attack me & tell me what she thinks, but she is too cunning to abuse me to others, when she knows she would be the Victim –

I think she must leave York; the good Belcombe's Kindness has been in this Case I fear misapplied, it would have been better for this malignant Wretch to have lived on unknown & unnoticed –

The day pours so with Rain that this Letter must remain another Day - which grieves me –

I have just read Mr D what I have said & he approves - need I say more for what he thinks? My feelings I know are quick & warm, but he is all Coolness, Moderation & Goodness.

I hope this will be the last letter to you containing a Syllable on so Odious a Subject.

Wednesday Morning - I wish you to tell Miss R that Mr D has told Mrs Duffin every thing she said to him & she immediately said she will never see her till she has asked Mr D's Pardon.

I wish you also to tell her that he knows from Mariana all the Reports of York respecting her & that their Kindness solely was the Cause of some few calling on her –

I will give you another Proof of my taking every Pain to hide her Conduct: all the Percivals drank Tea here the Day she left of Course poor Mrs D was full of the Commotion and told them all - when I returned from Nunmonkton the next day Mr D said he was sorry she had said any thing to them as it might injure the Girl - I went to Acomb, called on them & begged them not to mention the Circumstance, which they promised, & I believe very soon after called on her. It was more than 3 Weeks before I mentioned any thing to you & then I thought your Letter called upon me to be equally explicit.

181

Both dark-skinned illegitimate sisters had found that they were not wanted by English society except for their money, and as intelligent young women they reacted violently. In Jane's case her violence was directed towards herself; she had lost all pride and hedonistically gave herself to men for money since she had nothing more to look forward to. Eliza however was just approaching the depths of social debasement that her sister had been going through for the previous two years, and her reaction was outward;

she erupted with verbal condemnation of the Duffins whom she had once held close, followed by intense depression.

When Eliza returned to York Miss Marsh had already spread gossip about her around the town. Eliza was ostracised even more or else avoided. She pleaded with Anne for support but none was forthcoming. At Shibden Hall with Mariana Anne had finally found a soul mate so she cut herself off from Eliza's sordid affairs. A fortnight later Eliza sent yet another disappointed, cold, formal request for her belongings. Again Anne did not reply.

The following day Jane was finally found in London. Mr Dickenson took her into care and put her into a home in Woodford. She was acknowledged to be quite sane.

Eliza finally lost her temper. She asked Duffin the address of her uncle's widow in Scarborough, and sent it to Jane who made her way there. Duffin, felt Eliza, had no time for them now; he had more time for Miss Marsh who thought she was more mad than her sister, though Duffin saw her as merely malicious. She also asked for her will which he held on her behalf, then said goodbye to him forever before leaving for her own lodging. Unknown to him her will had been written in Anne Lister's favour when they expected to spend their lives together; there was no point in that any more.

When Jane arrived in Scarborough she took down the portrait of her father and shredded it into fine strips in her fury. He had ruined her life from the start: why had they been born bastards? Why did they have dark skins? What did England have to do with Madras? Why had they been parted from their mother who loved them? Why had their money not been held in trust permanently? How could he have made her a social misfit? Then, much quieter, she went off with a man; nobody else would pay for her food and lodging.

All of this was grist to Miss Marsh's mill:

Scarbro', Thursday Night Oct 20th 1814[182]

… Lady C's Manners I admire, but I daresay she might be distant to me, thinking me your & Miss R's friend – She retains great Dislike to both – She was astonished when Mr D told her of Miss R's behaviour to you as she looked upon you as the Golden Calf set up by Miss R to worship. She declined having anything to do with Miss R unless she makes an apology & was shocked at all her strange conduct to Mr D & her sister. She says Pride is & will be her ruin& an odd account she gave of her whilst at Doncaster; however as the one is as odd as the other we must not attend much to what is said by either.

Jane[183] cut her father's picture (that large one that you remember at York) in small shreds; whilst at Scarbro' she behaved quietly enough it appears, but very oddly, till at last she went off with that Fellow who called on Miss R at York last May. As I was not present when anything alluding to either was named I have heard only a few Things …

Mr D has had a letter from Mrs Boulton184, she is off from Woodford, [annoyed185] at her Sister beyond all bounds & angry at Mr Dickinson – but the Latter is perfectly Sane. I shall not be at all surprised at her coming to York again if it is only to plague her Sister, who I think will do well to quit a Place she has made herself so notorious in.

I seriously hope if She asks your advice you will give it for her speedy departure. I am pretty certain Mr D would like it. He sent her Will back last Monday in a blank Cover, he never said a Word of his Intentions & the next Day came a Note from her, I will recollect it as nearly as I can,

"My dear Sir, I received my Will which you sent me to Day & I beg you will accept my Thanks for having kept it so long. As this is probably the last letter you will receive from me I have only to assure you I shall ever feel myself your grateful Eliza."

This may not be exact but it is very near & I don't like to ask for it as Mr D said he should not take notice of it to any one.

…. I shall religiously observe a strict silence about her. I have promised & will keep my promise. I have raged at her to you, I have never to anyone else expressed anything but Pity. I have not been in York for nine or ten weeks …

Your faithfully & affectionately attached   MJM

"… I shall not be surprised to find she quits York forever, which I think would be a wise bet for she will not long have many friends there or perhaps anywhere. For kindness seems to make her hate people… What can all this be but diseasement or the want of a heart; or if she has one it is a black one…

I have done with her & all the black Progeny forever. Being now quite of my former opinion that where black blood is, there can be nothing amiable.

I sincerely wish Mr D was quit of them altogether, for he has nothing but trouble & vexation with the whole thing. Now an end to the odious subject…"

    Eliza, deeply distressed to be so maligned for protecting her sister, was reported by her servant to have lived on water for three weeks and to look wretched. In Miss Marsh's opinion she was deranged and something had to be done about her. She asked Anne to speak to Eliza, not understanding the depth of betrayal Eliza felt where Anne was concerned. Yet again Anne stayed in the background, though this time she did ask Mariana to go and visit her.

    Mariana asked for help from her father, with the result that Eliza was taken into his temporary care under Lady Crawfurd's guardianship at Clifton Green, the private Quaker asylum. As soon as she had calmed down and written an abject apology to Anne with a request for her Sacrament Book, still in Anne's possession, Eliza was once more declared sane.

But she was still undoubtedly very depressed.

She no longer had any faith in Anne, nor did she trust Mr Duffin or Miss Marsh. They did not seem to care any longer for her or for Jane; there was clearly nothing she could do about her sister's terrible predicament, and they would do nothing for either of them. Without the patronage or assistance of Anne or Mr Duffin, would her fate be the same as her sister's? Would she live alone on the streets with no friends or resources?

1815

For the next few months these thoughts rattled around Eliza's head, until in her grief, loneliness and isolation she once more began to be aggressive those around her. She was again admitted to Clifton Green, this time for an extended stay from May. Miss Marsh reported to Anne that Eliza was deranged and asked her to visit, but Anne, now seeing herself as the Lister heir, was deeply involved in her new affair with Mariana and her permanent move to Shibden Hall; she could not find time.

1816

By February 1816 Eliza was improving and was eventually released from Clifton Green.

Back in Blake Street she began to put her affairs in order, organising all of her possessions into two trunks.

She put in the things she least wanted to lose, like the love letters she and Captain Alexander had exchanged. When she read them again she understood that he really had loved her, that he really would have married her. He had obviously told her the truth while Anne had obviously lied to her by saying that she would live with Eliza when she was 21, then saying that he only wanted to marry her for her fortune.

Because she had believed Anne she had missed her chance of love and happiness with him.

She wrote out a new will and placed it carefully in the bottom of one of the trunks.

Meanwhile in York Mrs Belcombe had privately found a new suitor for Mariana. In early March 1816 she asked her daughter without fail to return to Petergate for a few days, saying that Anne, who normally accompanied Mariana everywhere, should stay three streets away with Mr Duffin in Micklegate because there was no room for her in Petergate. Mariana was then hastily transported to Stoke-on Trent to be married to Charles Lawton, a man of affluence about twenty years older. Her dowry was £6000.

Anne was devastated by such duplicity and astonished at such a betrayal by Mariana, but when her tears of outrage dried she visited the newly married couple along with Mariana's younger sister Anne (Nantz), at the marital home, Lawton Hall. Under Charles' nose she furtively resumed her clandestine affair with Mariana and also started a new one with Nantz. Nevertheless after five months a quarrel broke out, to do with a lock of Nantz's pubic hair that Anne had cut off. The two were quickly sent back to York and the affair fizzled out, despite promises of everlasting love.

On parting Anne made Mariana promise that they would live together in five years, when Charles was expected to die. Of course Mariana agreed.

In April or May 1816, after again attacking and screaming at those around her, Eliza was permanently committed to Dr Belcombe's private Clifton Green Asylum. But her emotional state had come under scrutiny, and Miss Marsh and Mr Duffin were beginning to realise more about her feelings of betrayal by Anne. They talked about them to Anne, who was now having to live without Mariana.

"From a little before tea till near 11 at night looking over poor Eliza Raine's letters. My heart bled at the remembrance of the past. Poor girl! She did indeed love me truly." [186]

Eliza's extreme mental pain had become more apparent to Mr Duffin and Miss Marsh, so they finally began to listen more carefully to what she was saying. When they belatedly understood the secret relationship between Anne and Eliza and the real source of Eliza's despair and depression, they put pressure on Anne to explain her actions:

"…Took a chaise to Miss Marsh's lodgings. She was at Mr Duffin's, and she and Mr Duffin came to give me the meeting. Not expecting to see him, his coming increased my agitation – I burst into tears and was obliged to leave the room a little and behaved very foolishly.

Miss Marsh (who had read my last letter to Mariana in which I alluded to the misunderstanding between Mr Duffin and me about the letter written to him by Eliza Raine, containing a copy of her will) mentioned it to Mr Duffin."

In December 1817 Anne was prevailed upon to visit her:

"She seemed pleased at my visit and expressed a wish for me to go again, which I promised. The first thing she said to me was "Well! So you are in mourning for your mother! Is your father going to marry again?"…She afterwards asked me to take off my hat, felt my face, asked if I ever wore false faces, and at last said she "believed it was really my face".

She then bade me take off my right-hand glove, and observing the thick, gold ring Mariana gave me, asked what I had done with the one I used to wear. Then, looking at my other hand, asked significantly after "all my friends". She asked me what I had done with the gold chain she gave me, and what with the pocket-handkerchiefs. I told her. When I said I never came to York without seeing her she answered, "What! Never?" and seemed much pleased when I answered "No! Never!"

Anne could not deny the logic of Eliza's questions or their relevance:

"She behaved (as she had done before) more idiotically than madly. At my request we were left a little by ourselves. At first she said she should take no insolence, no impertinence from me; that I had never done her any good, and if I was impertinent we should come to blows.

After a somewhat stern remonstrance on my part, she said I had always thought nothing of her; that I might have genius, I might have talent, but that I had made a bad use of them and indeed the world thought me a fool.

She then grew more kind and asked to feel my face, to pinch my nose and feel my eyes. She said she believed it really was my face, seemed pleased to see me, and desired me to sit by her on the sopha.

At this moment Mr Duffin & Mrs Clarkson, the housekeeper, returned and I took my leave.

Eliza had tears in her eyes – the only sensitive symptoms I have observed since her malady."
188

1817

Eliza was now isolated from the world. Nevertheless important news reached her from time to time. Sometime after June 11th she was told of the death of Jane's son, her own nephew aged 6.

1819

The wheel of fortune turned for Jane in 1819. When Lieutenant Henry Boulton was killed in action in Calcutta she was still married to him, and so inherited back all that he had not spent. About a thousand had disappeared, so with interest she was left about £3000. Unfortunately it was much too late; her son had died two years before and she now had a constant spitting of blood. She died of consumption189 in November aged 30, but looking 60. As her only relative Eliza inherited all her fortune.

When Jane died Eliza was taken away from Mr Duffin against his wishes, to be taken in with absolute determination by her cousin and legal guardian Lady Crawfurd. She dressed Eliza in black but had no wish to go into mourning herself. Her excuse was her distrust of Dr Belcombe. In early 1819 a scandal erupted at his Clifton Green Asylum:190

"A certain Miss Jane Horsman was admitted to the Asylum at the request of a relative, Rev. William Bulmer, on the grounds that she was suffering from suicidal tendencies and was not safe to be at large. In less than a month Miss Horsman, whose symptoms at this distance in time seemed to bear some resemblance to those of dipsomania, was apparently cured and due for discharge on Wednesday 3rd June, when a certificate of sanity was to be signed and she should be returned to the care of her mother.

On hearing she was to be discharged her relatives, the Bulmers, were alarmed, why is not clear, and approached a magistrate, Mr Dickens (who was by the way a barrister and legal adviser to the Asylum) to have her released at once.

This Mr Dickens achieved by the extraordinary method of calling with a closed carriage and a set of blacksmith's tools and breaking down the Asylum door while both medical men were off duty and the house in charge of the Matron.

Miss Horsman was then abducted – under protest, by the Matron's account – leaving all concerned in a welter of counter-accusations and threatened actions at law.

It is impossible to disentangle the rights and wrongs of this strange incident, possibly turning on some extraneous circumstance such as Miss Horsman's fortune, her future marriage (she was quite a young woman) or a quarrel between her relatives and her mother.

The peculiar and hasty action of Mr Dickens is made more odd by "*the particular intimacy between him and Dr Belcombe.*"

After hearing this Lady Crawfurd was appalled that Eliza was held under Dr Belcombe's care in such a '*disreputable*' asylum. She therefore insisted on lodging Eliza privately in a rented house in Gillygate in the centre of York. Despite Duffin threatening to wash his hands of Eliza forever, and Miss Marsh saying it was one maniac looking after another, Lady C. would brook no refusal. In this place there were no "*insanes*" so Eliza could recover in peace with the help of a widow and her three daughters.

At this time Eliza was still possession of most of her original £4000, less furniture bought in Halifax, rent in Hot Wells and York, and travelling costs, which amounted to £500 at the most. However in the last few years she had had no opportunity to spend any of it or the interest of about £200 per annum, though the cost of the asylum was probably about £50 annually. After Jane's death she had inherited two or three thousand more plus interest, if declared sane. Altogether it would amount to about £7550.

Lady Crawfurd was extremely happy to care for Eliza, who suddenly recovered her senses while Jane's will was being settled.

But unfortunately it was soon decided that no money would devolve to Lady C, whereupon Eliza had a sudden relapse and had to be hastily sent back to Clifton Green asylum.

Nevertheless, during the gap in his guardianship Mr Duffin made progress in his private life with a little help from Miss Marsh. Anne, residing at his house while she continued her studies at the Manor School, was a witness:

"I was sitting on the table reading with my back to them & never once looked round. There was sitting on his knee & open-mouthed kissing. I fancied from his manner of breathing & from circumstances altogether that he had his hand up her petticoats.

After tea…backgammon with Mrs Duffin…

Miss Marsh went to the Salmonds a little after 6…very much in the amoroso…She kissed me & put her tongue to my lips.

I almost involuntarily called out God bless me. Kept wiping my lips. Said I had never had such a kiss before and it was the oddest sensation in the world. We all laughed most heartily. In opening the front door, she gave me another such kiss, saying, can you not put your tongue between your lips? shewing me how. I said no, it was such an odd sensation it set my teeth on edge."

1820

In May 1820 Duffin resumed his guardianship of Eliza. Her behaviour had become erratic and violent though she did have "*lucid intervals*". She was formally certified insane pending sustained improvement.

It was therefore necessary to take power of attorney. Duffin had always looked after her trust fund during her childhood. Now that she was 29 it was just as easy to pay her bills and guard the capital. He sent her clothes to Lady Crawfurd to keep, along with her silver ornaments and other trinkets and a full inventory "*to be forthcoming when called for*", and sent a letter to Anne to enquire about the items that Eliza said she still possessed. Naturally Anne was preoccupied:

"Tib 1820 Oct Tues 17   9 ½

Very stormy, windy night – Miss V   191 came to call us about eight & a half till after nine in bed between us at Tib's192 & my particular request, I pressing her as well as I could for Tib not to know.

In the course of the morning she came into my room for my gloves to mend, sat on my knee & staid half an hour, both of us in a state of great excitement. I told her I did not like to waste her feelings & it was very foolish when we could have no opportunity, said I was not well & should not be till I had been with her again etc., said I had writ two or three answers to the letter I had from her last February tenth before I could get my answer cool enough etc.

I see I may say & do what I like.

I wished this house was my own for six days & Tib with Madame Mettineus. What! said she, only six days? You would be tired of me then? I reassured her etc. etc.

A very affectionate letter from Mariana this morning makes my heart ache, she exhorts me so sweetly to carefulness & constancy. I think had her letter come sooner I could & should have withstood this girl.

She wrote to Mrs Milne about Edward's breaking his leg as if nothing had happened between them & asked her opinion of Miss Vallance. She replies 'You ask me how I like Miss Vallance – I begin to think I must give way to Louisa's opinion – she is plausible but I neither fancy her sincere nor honest, but perhaps I judge prematurely – if I return to Langton I will tell you more about her.'

Poor Mariana, she will never know half my follies. Oh may she never and if we ever come together I will do my utmost to make her happy. I do love her as I have never loved before unless Eliza were once excepted. I will reform & be constant, I will hope to be more what I should be.

Her letter sticks to my heart but alas she is away from me and I am weak against the arts of this understanding practiser of blandishment. She is a deep I am half persuaded but she shall get nothing out of me farther [than] she has done. I will play her own game, she excites my passion but in fact as for regard as connected with esteem I cannot feel a particle of it and even as to other things she is full ready enough.

Very kind letter from M (Lawton) forwarded from York by Mr D - L193 is far from well, his constitution much broke of late and they live like brother and sister as to platonics –

Oh that M and I could be together, I would indeed be steady, but heaven knows my deserts and mine iniquity. Oh that I were better.

Letter from my Aunt, Shibden. My uncle sent on Saturday exactly what I had written to accept Mr Bilton's proposal to buy Pump194 at five thousand guineas – if it can be got over tolerably I am glad, at all events my present feeling is satisfaction.

Miss Vallance has been in again with my gloves which she has mended."
195

Very much embarrassed, Anne explained to Mr Duffin that she no longer had Eliza's diamond ring: perhaps it had been turned into a pair of diamond earrings? She admitted that Eliza's portrait of William Raine, and his will in Eliza's handwriting were still in her possession; but she omitted to mention other things Duffin might not be aware of. However, she argued, was it right and just that a guardian should have all his ward's possessions in his own care? After all, Eliza had given her these things to look after when she was sane. Shouldn't Anne keep them for her in case she recovered?

Meanwhile Duffin was occupied with the contents of Eliza's two trunks. He had found the documents that Eliza had stored there whilst sane. For the first time he read the bundle of letters between her and Captain Alexander, then he wrote down his final opinion before burning them:

"…What a melancholy reflection that a young Creature should have been thrown into so hazardous a situation! And the consequences ever to be deplored! His letters and her replies too fully explain what happened during those midnight meetings but all is now buried in oblivion as the whole has been committed to the flames."
196

He also found the will that Eliza had made, leaving her fortune to Captain Alexander. She had written it when she was not in the asylum, so it would be difficult to dismiss as invalid. In any case whilst in the asylum she had also written lucidly. He sent it to his lawyer, Jonathan Gray to be assessed.

Meanwhile he allowed Anne to keep what Eliza had given her, not only the things she had mentioned to him but also the morocco pocket-case, two ivory syringes, the diaries and copious other letters and documents, which Anne filed carefully in her room at home.

So things continued for another eleven years.

1825

In 1825 Mrs Louisa Duffin died, after which Miss Marsh married Mr Duffin within a few months.

1831 - 1840

Anne visited Clifton Green Asylum intermittently, her visits always provoking strong feelings in both Eliza and herself.

She noted her visits in code in her diary: in 1831 she found Eliza contrary but relatively quiet and clean, despite her receding gums, dirty habits and incoherence. Now that Lady Crawfurd had died and Mr Duffin was over 80 the trust had hired a new personal guardian for her, Miss Wilson.

Through the passing years Eliza's physical health remained good. In 1832, aged 41, she escaped the violent cholera epidemic that swept through York; although twelve months later her dresses sprouted straitjacket sleeves to prevent her from hitting out violently at visitors.

In 1835 she was removed to another room *"where she is under some control"*. The same year Duffin asked Jonathan Gray to have a last look at her papers to see if anything could be done about the will.

A year later, after much badgering by Mrs Duffin, Mr Gray wearily stated that he could find no evidence to validate the will. The elderly gentlewoman was irritated that Eliza, now aged 45, should be "*happy*", healthy and "*most likely to outlive us all*" but that her vast fortune could not be made available to those who could use it. Eighteen months later her health and looks had improved further, so attempts were made to find her erstwhile servant Grace Whinray, to whom Eliza had left ten pounds in her will.

In 1838 Mr Duffin died aged 93. His widow continued to visit Eliza.

In 1840 Anne was on a tour of Russia and reached Tbilisi in Georgia. The summer weather was blisteringly hot, and great precautions were taken regarding water and food. Nevertheless Anne was bitten by an insect and died of a virus infection within three days.

Her constant companion was now Miss Anne Walker, a nervous spinster heiress from Halifax who had insisted on travelling because she hated the whisperings of Yorkshire society concerning their relationship. After Anne's death she was compelled to transport the body all the way back to Shibden Hall. Anne had bequeathed her a life interest in Shibden Hall, but lawyers of the next Lister heirs in Wales were not in agreement. Whilst fighting them on paper for the next eleven years Miss Walker became a melancholy recluse in Anne's mansion; finally papers were served and she too was forcibly committed to an asylum.

1840 - 1860

In 1841 Dr Henry Belcombe retired and was succeeded by his son Dr Stephen Belcombe, who inherited the Quaker asylum in Clifton Green and its 12 male and 14 female inmates. Isabella Clarkson, the matron, now aged 60, soon retired.

The new matron, Mary Ann King, continued her work until 1853, by which time the asylum had dwindled to only a handful of residents. That year Dr Stephen Belcombe retired and sold the building to a schoolteacher, who turned it into a boys' school.

Eliza, still a permanent inmate, had quietened over the years as the world ceased to hurt her. She was moved to the Terrace House, a private residence in the village of Osbaldwick, east of York. Here she had no relatives or loved ones, no friends or acquaintances except her nurse and housekeeper, Hannah Keable, and the man who did the house maintenance.

Seven years later in 1860 she suffered a stomach haemorrhage and died, aged 68. Her death was registered on the 5th of January 1861.

By that time her fortune had increased to £8000[1]. As she was a bastard (an illegitimate child) with no relatives, and also an inmate of a mental asylum, she could not make a will. As her previous will had been declared invalid by her solicitor, Jonathan Grey, her money was claimed by the Crown.

> ON the 29th day of November 1861, Letters of Administration of all and singular the personal Estate and Effects of Eliza Raine ~~formerly of~~ ~~and~~ late of Osbaldwick in the County of York deceased, who died on the 31st day of December 1860 at Osbaldwick aforesaid a Spinster and a Bastard were granted at the Principal Registry of Her Majesty's Court of Probate to Henry Revell Reynolds of the Treasury Chambers Whitehall in the County of Middlesex Esquire Solicitor for the affairs of Her Majesty's Treasury and his Successors in the said Office for the use of Her Majesty ~~of the~~ ~~said deceased~~ he having been first sworn duly to administer ~~and next of Kin of the said deceased, having first renounced or having survived the said deceased, but died without having taken upon the Letters of Administration of personal Estate and Effects~~.
>
> By Motion & Decree.
>
> Effects under £8000.

She was given a quiet funeral fit for a gentlewoman, and buried just across the road from where she had lived, in the grounds of the Church of St Thomas in Osbaldwick, as a token of what Hannah Keable felt for her.

Her grave is still there today, and the stone as clean as if erected yesterday.

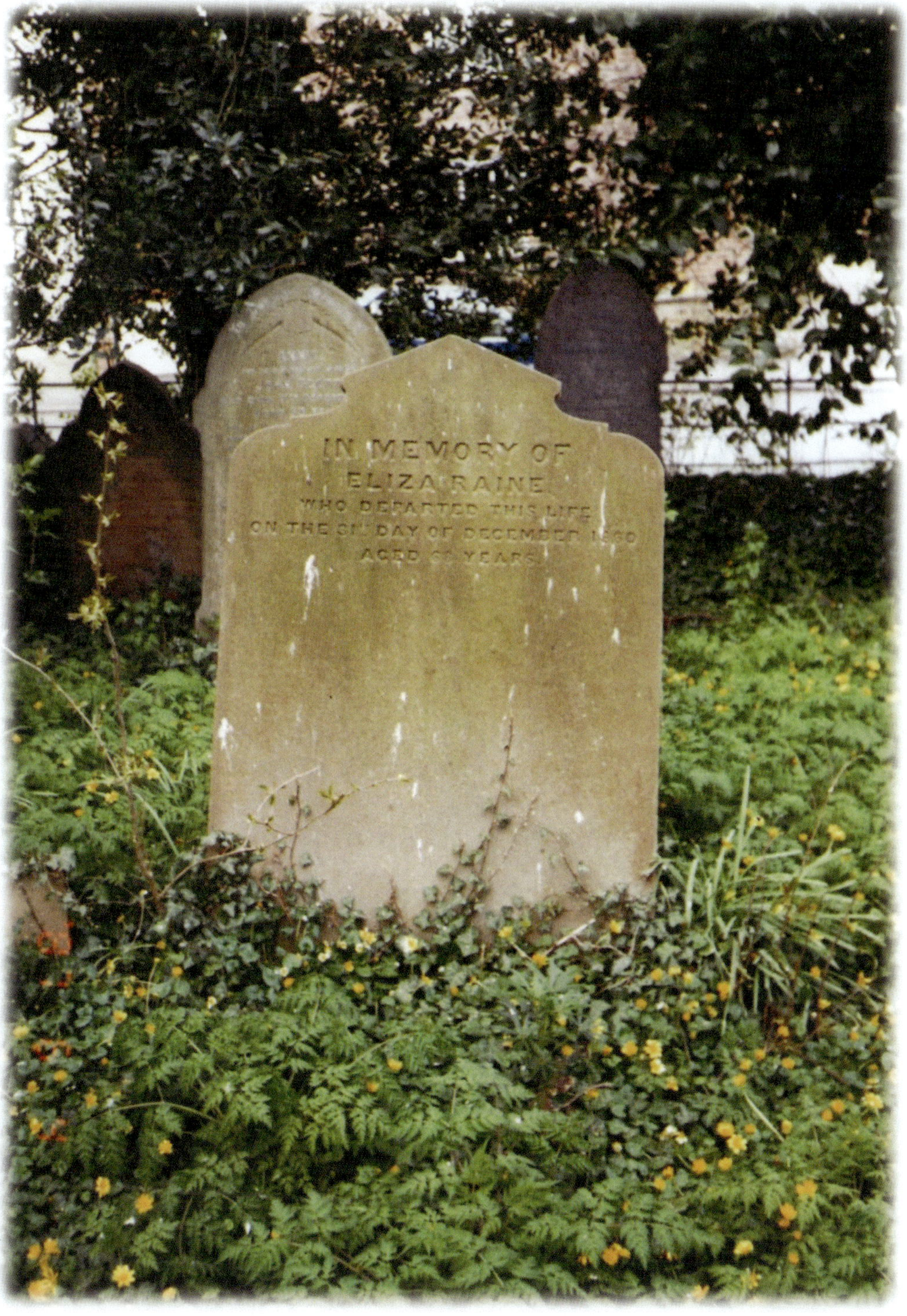
IN MEMORY OF
ELIZA RAINE
WHO DEPARTED THIS LIFE

Pupils at the Manor School, 1805 written by Anne or Eliza

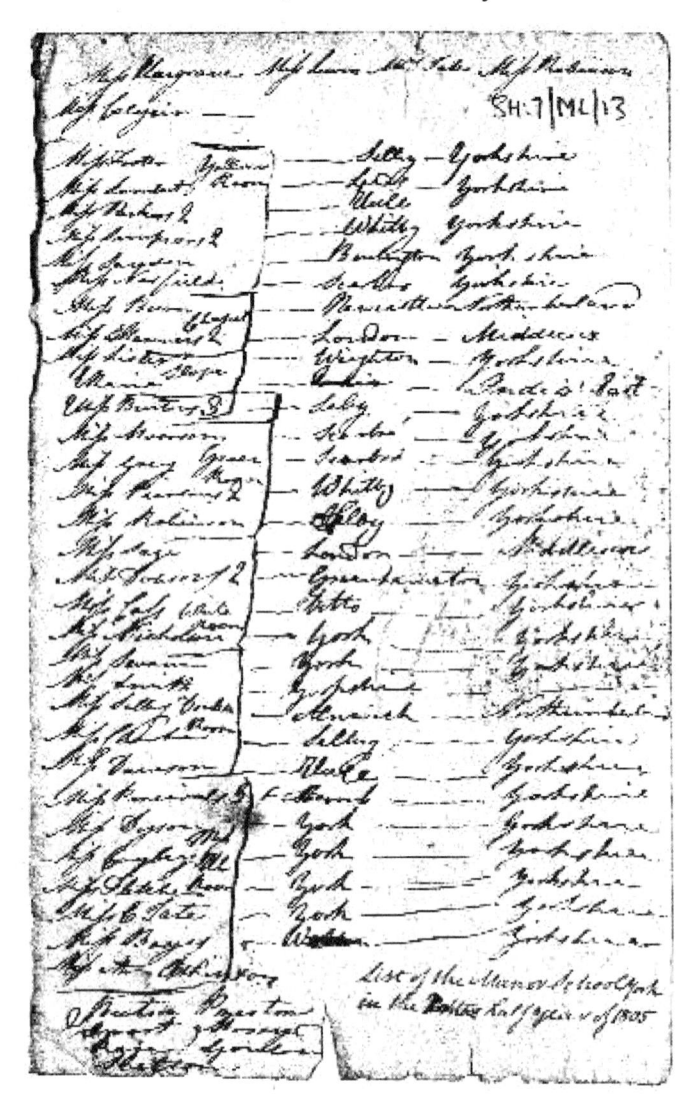

Part of the Family Obituary for Samuel Lister, written by his sister Anne

Died SH:3/LF/28/9

19th June at Fermoy, Samuel Lister Esq. of the 84th Reg.t — aged 20, only son of Jer.h Lister Esq.r of Halifax. The melancholy accident which cut off in the prime of life, this truly excellent young man must ever stamp his loss with double force upon the hearts of his disconsolate family & afflicted friends. He went out with some of his brother officers to bathe in the Blackwater — scarcely had he plunged in before the current forced him from his depth — his friend saw him sink beyond the power of assistance — and oh! he sunk to rise no more — Tho' every exertion was immediately made, the body was not found till it had been 2 hours under water — All means to restore life proved ineffectual, his sainted spirit had escaped for ever, & had left all those, who knew him to lament & regret his loss. He was the best of sons, of brothers, & of friends and lastly it is all the worthy tribute they can pay —

A note in code written by Anne or Eliza [SH:7/ML/E/26]

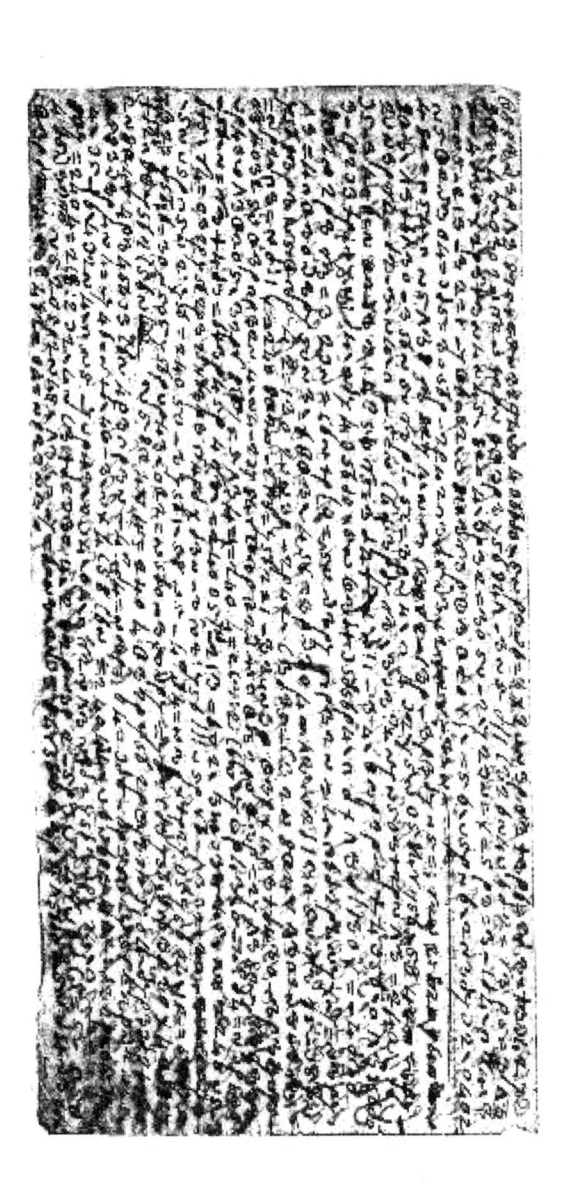

Shibden Hall, home of Anne Lister in Halifax, Yorkshire, UK

Notes

[1] Dictionary of National Biography (DNB)
[2] William Raine's will
[3] SH:3/LF/1-29
[4] Madras Inventories 1802/3, L/AG/34/29/203ff. 139-44
[5] SH:7/ML/7
[6] SH:7/ML/13 gives a list of all pupils. Most boarders (39 in total) were from Yorkshire, two were from Northumberland and two were from Middlesex. Many were sisters. In addition there were 7 day pupils including Jane Raine.
[7] SH:7/LL.344 dated 15th August 1805.
[8] SH:7/ML/8
[9] Twelve for a girl, fourteen for a boy.
[10] Until 1870 anything of value owned by a woman e.g. wages, investment, gift or inheritance automatically became the property of her husband on marriage. Married women had hardly any legal rights separate from their husbands and were not recognized in law. In contrast single and widowed women were 'feme sole', i.e. independent woman, and had the right to own property.
[11] SH:7/ML/A/1
[12] Altogether various odd sheets, three notebooks and 23 volumes of Anne Lister's diaries are held at Calderdale Archives, Yorkshire.
[13] John Dalton FRS (6 September 1766 – 27 July 1844) was an English chemist, meteorologist and physicist.
[14] Rebecca Lister's adopted son from Ireland.
[15] The local vicar and schoolteacher.
[16] Mane = Greek 'blood', so probably the onset of menstruation.
[17] Where Rebecca Lister's mother owned a farm.
[18] The mail = the post coach.
[19] The music teacher
[20] A plain black riding skirt
[21] SH:7/ML/A/4
[22] = Gk: much blood: a heavy menstrual period.
[23] Her period?
[24] Northgate House in the centre of Halifax was the home of her uncle Joseph and Aunt Lister, who were childless. They were both older than Captain Lister, Anne's father. In the 20th century their house became the largest hotel in the town.
[25] Ten shillings and sixpence.
[26] With Anne as her flute teacher.
[27] SH/7/ML/A/8
[28] Shibden Hall in Halifax was the home of Anne's uncle James Lister and his unmarried siblings including Aunt Anne. The youngest sibling was Captain Jeremy Lister, Anne's father.
[29] Lewis Alexander, a young boy in a local family in Halifax. Miss A was his sister.
[30] Alexander

[31] Ellen Royd or The Royd, home of the Rawson family, local bankers.
[32] Book 4
[33] Esquire
[34] The Duffins' country house in Nunmonkton outside York.
[35] Rev. Dr. Andrew Bell, Eliza's mathematics tutor and later founder of Bell's National Schools.
[36] Boulton.
[37] SH:7/ML/A/8
[38] James Raine married Mary Pennock on 23rd January 1798 and had son James and twins Stephen and David, born 1799 and 1801. Mary probably died in childbirth. He married Mary Barker on 31st January 1804 and had William, Mary, Ann, Seth and Enos. All were christened in Seamer near Scarborough. IGI.
[39] French Revolution 1787 - 99
[40] *Letters from France in 1802* by Henry Redhead Yorke in 2 vols. London 1804
[41] A rout was a party in modern parlance.
[42] Eliza Raine's diary.
[43] Dr Hunter was chief medical officer at York Lunatic Asylum
[44] Anne Lister's Notebook for March 1808.
[45] International Genealogical Index
[46] During the Regency evening parties were much the rage. The word rout, synonymous with large unruly gatherings, soon came to mean a fashionable assembly, or large evening party.
[47] SH:7/ML/A/12
[48] Eliza currently called Anne "Welly" after Wellington.
[49] Nuptials?
[50] SH:7/ML/A/13/6 written by Eliza with addendum by Anne. N = nuptials?
[51] A woman being alone with a man often caused "breach of promise" i.e. the man would claim that a woman had privately agreed to marry him and then publicly withdrawn, thereby allowing him to claim substantial damages at law.
[52] J10.12.1808
[53] J14.12.1808
[54] J16.12.1808
[55] Now a museum, Shibden Hall in Halifax was the home of the Lister family from ca 1500. Anne's uncle James had inherited the house and looked after his unmarried sisters there, including aunt Anne who was paying for young Anne's education.
[56] SH/7/ML/A/13/5 Written by Eliza.
[57] Dropped her from their social circle.
[58] J10.03.09
[59] J20.03.09
[60] J22.03.09
[61] J28.03.09
[62] J 8.4.09
[63] J 8.5.09
[64] SH:7/ML/A/11
[65] The elderly physician Dr Hunter had been in charge of York Insane Asylum, and was a friend of Anne Lister's aunt of the same name.
[66] To their residence, Red House, in Nunmonkton, a village outside York, in order to be at a distance from cholera, typhoid and other diseases common in York during the summer.

[67] With her husband Henry Boulton who was rejoining his regiment.

Notebook SH:7/ML/A/13/1
[70] India Office Records, British Library. Madras Officer Services L/MIL/11/67
[71] J 24.1.10
[72] Ibid
[73] DNB
[74] SH:7/ML/A/15 Anne wrote on the envelope: "*written ver. soon aft. E.R. went to reside wth Lady C. at Doncaster early in Ap. (proby.) 1810.*"
[75] SH:7/ML/A/16
[76] Jane's lawyer in London.
[77] Workhouses had not yet been invented.
[78] SH:7/ML/A/20
[79] SH:7/ML/A/19
[80] SH:7/ML/A/23
[81] SH:7/ML/A/24
[82] Anne's new friend at school.
[83] "Ends" refers to writing only on the ends of the letter.
[84] The pelisse was a type of coat made of cloth worn over a dress or gown, either as an outdoor garment or for indoor or evening wear.
[85] A regular coach
[86] SH:7/ML/A/25
[87] SH:7/ML/A/25
[88] SH:7/ML/A/28
[89] Shibden Hall
[90] now bankrupt
[91] ditto
[92] Anne's youngest brother, the Lister family heir. He wanted to join the Army.
[93] The earliest bank in Halifax, the commercial Bank of Hainsworth, Holden, Swaine and Pollard, was established in 1779 as it became less reliant on Leeds. Swaine was a worsted manufacturer. Cloth sales gave him funds in London where he and his brother owned a bank. The commercial Bank became Brothers Swaine & Co. but collapsed in 1807 with some £64,000 outstanding in banknotes, and £42,000 in drafts. Swaine's worsted business survived. The remains of Swaine's bank passed to major creditors John Rawson, John Rhodes and Rawdon Briggs who formed a successor bank until 1811, when the partnership split. Rhodes and Briggs, both mill owners, continued as Halifax Bank and they were later joined by John Garlick, previously a clerk at Swaines. The Rawson family started a new bank with a branch at Huddersfield. Both firms prospered.

[94] Joint Stock Companies Act 1844 and Limited Liability Act 1855.
[95] SH:7/ML/A/26/1
[96] Regular coaches to York.
[97] Anne's schoolfriend's brother in the army was lost at war.
[98] Mr & Mrs Whitaker and Mrs Percival were teachers at the Manor school.
[99] L 29.7.10

[100] SH:7/ML/A/25
[101] SH:7/ML/E/26
[102] SH:7/ML/Aug 18th 1810
[103] SH:7/ML/A/28
[104] SH:7/ML/A/29
[105] By contrast, the average pay of a servant was £10 per annum.
[106] SH:7/ML/A/30

[108] Hebden Bridge
[109] English Dissenters were Christians who separated from the Established Church from the 16th century. They originally campaigned for a Protestant reformation of the Church of England.
[110] This could mean Zelus, the son of Pallas and Styx in Greek mythology.
[111] Ps means sex
[112] Passage in code deleted.
[113] The first letter of the surname is illegible.
[114] Code A
[115] SH:7/ML/A/30
[116] Hannah Lister, elderly sister to James, Anne (snr), Joseph and Jeremy, also resident at Shibden Hall as an unmarried spinster.
[117] Priestley, Rawson, Walker, Paley and Saltmarshe families were very affluent in commerce, trade or banking.
[118] Enlisting in the Army.
[119] Illegible
[120] due to bankruptcy
[121] Illegible
[122] i.e. for financial means
[123] The Napoleonic Wars were in full swing, so France was to be avoided at all costs. The Peninsular War 1808-14: Wellington had just defeated Massena at Fuentes d'Onoro on May 5th 1811, and Beresford defeated Soult at Albuera on May 16th 1811, so Almeida, the last fortress in Portugal held by the French under Napoleon was captured by the British. With Portugal cleared of the French a base of attack was established on the long lines of the French from Madrid to Bayonne.
[124] Irish niece of Mr Duffin, also a pupil at the Manor School. Paid for by her uncle, she expected no dowry and was to return to Ireland as a governess.
[125] code
[126] Her period.
[127] SH:7/ML/A/31
[128] Four shillings
[129] The Lusiad of Luis Camoens; English translation by William Julius Mickle in 1776.
[130] SH:7/ML/A/32 A note sent to Anne Lister while she was on holiday from the Manor school & resident at North Bridge. The poem that follows was written on the reverse.
[131] Possibly an acknowledgement of an earlier spelling error: "dyed".
[132] SH:7/ML/A/66
[133] Barbara Hutton: Clifton and its People in the Nineteenth Century.
[134] SH:7/ML/A/35

[135] Captain John Alexander, youngest brother of Maria and Disney, whom Eliza had visited extensively in company with Anne two years before and had remained in contact with since. He knew her well and was aware of her personal circumstances.
[136] Halifax
[137] Eliza will have her 21st birthday in 6 weeks and will then come into her £4000 fortune.
[138] Anne Lister's annotation for filing.
[139] SH:7/ML/A/38
[140] Written by Capt A (John Alexander).
[141] SH:7/ML/A/44
[142] Ibid
[143] Ibid
[144] SH:7/ML/A/45
[145] SH:7/ML/A/47
[146] SH:7/ML/A/49 & 50
[147] Note written on letter by Anne Lister
[148] SH:7/ML/A/40
[149] SH:7/ML/A/43
[150] SH:7/ML/A/48
[151] The East Riding of Yorkshire, a county division.
[152] Eliza reached her 21st birthday without marrying, so she now has inherited her father's legacy of £4000, making her a rich and independent woman.
[153] Parties, in current parlance.
[154] SH:7/ML/A52
[155] ???
[156] SH:7/ML/A/59
[157] SH:7/ML/A/63
[158] SH:7/ML/A/65
[159] I.N. = Isabella Norcliffe, i.e. Tib.
[160] SH:7/ML/E/26
[161] Diary of Caroline Walker, June 28th 1813
[162] Ibid July 7th 1813
[163] By Thomas Cole.
[164] I.N. = Isabella Norcliffe. SH:7/ML/53, August-September 1814
[165] illegible
[166] illegible
[167] illegible
[168] illegible
[169] Shorthand for Anne Lister
[170] Mr James was in charge of their affairs at Coutts Bank.
[171] Jane's solicitor.
[172] SH:7/ML/A/88
[173] SH:7/ML/58. Late Sept. 1814.
[174] To singe = to burn

[176] Scarborough. Presumably she had gone to visit her brother and his family. Why he was not involved in Jane's and Eliza's problems is not clear. However it may be that he was ill.

[177] SH:7/ML/61
[178] The maid
[179] Devil?
[180] Lie?
[181] SH:7/ML/61
[182] SH:7/ML/63
[183] Eliza's sister
[184] Eliza's sister
[185] This word was erased; the suggested word is my own invention.
[186] Anne Lister's diary Sat 18th Oct. 1817
[187] Anne Lister's diary Wed. 10th Dec. 1817
[188] Ibid Thurs. 18th Dec. 1817
[189] tuberculosis
[190] Hutton, Barbara: Clifton and its People in the Nineteenth Century: a North Riding Township Now Part of York City. York; Yorkshire Philosophical Society 1969.
[191] Miss Vallance
[192] Isabella Norcliffe's
[193] Lawton
[194] Pump Farm
[195] Anne Lister's diary
[196] SH:7/ML/93 There had obviously been a sexual context to these late-night meetings, which must have been provoked by Captain Alexander since Eliza was very proper about such things. Thus he probably was attempting to marry her because of her fortune at 21. Whether he was in love with her is therefore immaterial.

Printed in Poland
by Amazon Fulfillment
Poland Sp. z o.o., Wrocław